ALL THINGS NEW

A DISCIPLESHIP MINISTRY FOR LIFE TRANSFORMATION

WORKBOOK

All scripture quotations, unless otherwise indicated, are taken from the New King James Version®. Copyright © 1982 by Thomas Nelson, Inc. Used by permission. All rights reserved. Scripture quotations marked NIV are taken from the HOLY BIBLE, NEW INTERNATIONAL VERSION ® Copyright © 1973, 1978, 1984 Biblica. Used by permission of Zondervan. All rights reserved. Scripture quotations marked KJV are taken from the King James Version. Public domain.

All Things New: A Discipleship Ministry for Life Transformation
All Things New Workbook

ISBN : 978-1-943852-98-7

Printed in the United States of America.

Copyright ©2018 by Debora Barr
DBarrMinistries@gmail.com
www.DBarrMinistries.org

True Potential, Inc.
PO Box 904
Travelers Rest, SC 29690
www.truepotentialmedia.com

No part of this book may be reproduced or transmitted in any form or by any means, electronic or mechanical, including photocopying, recording or by any information storage and retrieval system, without permission in writing from the publisher.

Contents

ABOUT THE AUTHOR 5
INTRODUCTION 7

The Word is Life 9
LESSON #1 HOMEWORK 9
LESSON #1 CLASSROOM DISCUSSION 15

The Enemy's Lies vs. God's Truth 17
LESSON #2 HOMEWORK 17
LESSON #2 CLASSROOM DISCUSSION 24

Freedom in Truth 26
LESSON #3 HOMEWORK 26
LESSON #3 CLASSROOM DISCUSSION 37

Hearing God's Voice 39
LESSON #4 HOMEWORK 39
LESSON #4 CLASSROOM DISCUSSION 50

Prayer – Communicating with God 52
LESSON #5 HOMEWORK 52
LESSON #5 CLASSROOM DISCUSSION 64

Fall of Man Root Causes of Sin 66
LESSON #6 HOMEWORK 66
TIMELINE/ROOT CAUSE EXERCISE 72
LESSON #6 CLASSROOM DISCUSSION 77

Forgiveness 79
LESSON #7 HOMEWORK 79
LESSON #7 CLASSROOM DISCUSSION 89
LESSON #7 IN-CLASS EXERCISE 90

Sexual Integrity 93
LESSON #8 HOMEWORK 93
LESSON #8 CLASSROOM DISCUSSION 107

Spiritual Warfare 110
LESSON #9 HOMEWORK 110
LESSON #9 CLASSROOM DISCUSSION 123

The Heart 125
LESSON #10 HOMEWORK 125
LESSON #10 CLASSROOM DISCUSSION 137

Our Authority in Christ to Rout Demons 139
LESSON #11 HOMEWORK 139
LESSON #11 CLASSROOM DISCUSSION 150

Forgiveness – Part II 152
LESSON #12 HOMEWORK 152
LESSON #12 CLASSROOM DISCUSSION 161

Removing Hindrances to Effective Prayer 163
LESSON #13 HOMEWORK 163

Prayer Blockers Possible Reasons Why Our Prayers Are Not Answered by God 174
LESSON #13 IN-CLASS SMALL GROUP EXERCISE 174

Holy Spirit's Power for Inner Healing and Sanctification 177
LESSON #14 HOMEWORK 177

Listening and Inner Healing Prayer 191
LESSON #15 HOMEWORK 191

The Power of Sharing Your Testimony 202
LESSON #16 HOMEWORK 202

Exposing the Pain and Glorifying God 215
LESSON #17 HOMEWORK 215
LESSON #17 IN-CLASS EXERCISE 226

Tailoring Your Message for the Listener 228
LESSON #18 HOMEWORK 228
LESSON #18 IN-CLASS EXERCISE 239

Spiritual Gifts and Calling 241
LESSON #19 HOMEWORK 241

Witnessing – The Great Commission 250
LESSON #20 HOMEWORK 250

Your Life's Purpose 262
LESSON #21 HOMEWORK 262

Testimony Development 275
LESSON #22 HOMEWORK 275

Personal Plan to Continue Daily Devotional 286
LESSON #23 HOMEWORK 286
TESTIMONY DEVELOPMENT AND SHARING 297
FINAL THOUGHTS 298

Answers to In-Class Discussions 299

ABOUT THE AUTHOR

The All Things New Ministry was born out of my transition out of nearly two decades of homosexuality through the love and support of a women's ministry Bible study group and the leadership of a church that was not willing to compromise their convictions while continuing to welcome and embrace me. If homosexuality is not your life-controlling issue, please know that this Discipleship Ministry will help you just like it helped me! God's Word changes lives no matter what areas of brokenness you have in your life! When I first began attending the church that started the transformation in my life, I had not yet accepted Jesus Christ as my Lord and Savior and I was happy living my life as a lesbian. I knew 'about' Jesus and what He did for me, and even labeled myself as a Christian, but I had not yet surrendered my whole life to Him. I had also been involved in a gay church for many years where I was indoctrinated in gay-theology, which affirmed my lifestyle as a part of the gay community. I was still living my life the way I wanted to, and that included being in a committed lesbian relationship with the woman I loved.

Once I fully surrendered my life to Jesus Christ, I began to regularly read the Bible and pray that God would reveal areas of sin in my life that I needed to repent of and turn away from. It was through my study of the Word of God that I realized that many areas of my life did not line up with His Word. As God revealed areas of sin, I repented and asked for his forgiveness, and He began to change me from the inside out. Only when the Scriptures guide your conduct, does transformation begin in your life. When I finally realized that God did not approve of my choice to live as a lesbian, I decided to turn away from homosexuality and live a life in a way that was pleasing to Him. The transition was not easy, and I relied heavily on the women in my Bible study who supported me with unconditional love and prayed for me as I turned away from the gay community, which had been my support structure for many years. I had to walk away from a relationship with the woman that I loved and we had to unravel our lives that we had previously intertwined together.

My prayer is that every person who is disconnected from God will establish an intimate relationship with Jesus Christ that completely transforms their life for all of eternity. His love is everlasting and completely satisfying – it is unlike anything we can ever experience in human relationships. I never knew that I wasn't living my best life until I was able to experience His love as I aligned my life with His Word. Jesus makes all things new!

Therefore, if anyone is in Christ, he is a new creation; old things have passed away; behold, all things have become new. (2 Corinthians 5:17 NKJV)

Contact the author:
Debora Barr
www.DBarrMinistries.org
DBarrMinistries@gmail.com

INTRODUCTION

ALL THINGS NEW: A DISCIPLESHIP MINISTRY FOR HEALING is a Bible Study and Discipleship Ministry for all people who are disconnected from a personal intimate relationship with Jesus Christ and are not experiencing the abundant life that is promised in the Bible to all who surrender their whole lives to the Lordship of Jesus Christ. It is designed to be facilitated by lay leaders who have a heart for God. The purpose of the All Things New Ministry is to aid in the spiritual healing and growth of people who are hungry for life transformation. This ministry is designed to help release people from the bondage of sin and to allow them to experience healing from the effects of having their lives separated or distant from God..

Each lesson contains five days of homework to be completed by the ministry participants prior to meeting as a group to discuss the lesson and complete the in-class exercises. Another very important aspect of this ministry is the weekly memory Scripture that relates to the lesson for the week.

If you are completing this workbook on your own and not using it as a part of a facilitated weekly Bible study, you will need to purchase the companion Facilitator Guide in order to have access to all of the material you need to get the most out of this Bible Study. This is especially relevant to the in-class exercises presented in this workbook. If you don't have the Facilitator Guide, or someone who is facilitating this Bible Study that is using that Facilitator Guide, some of the exercises may not make sense.

ACCOUNTABILITY PARTNERS

We grow spiritually as Christians by sharing our lives with other Christians. One important aspect of this Ministry is for you to have a trusted Christian Accountability Partner to share your journey with as you work through the homework assignments and weekly lessons. There will be times as you work through this material that you may feel like giving up or giving in to temptations that have been gripping you for years. Having an Accountability Partner who you can reach out to in times of temptation, or when you need a friend who understands what you are going through, can really help you to stay the course and experience victory over your struggles.

You may be assigned an Accountability Partner by the Ministry Facilitator(s) to work with you, or if you are completing this workbook on your own, please find someone who you trust; who you feel comfortable talking to; and who you can contact when you have questions or are struggling to complete an assignment. That person's role is to encourage you and to pray for you. Stay in regular contact with your Accountability Partner – sharing the homework assignments with them and letting them know how you are feeling as you work through this material.

OTHER RESOURCES FOR COMPLETION OF THIS COURSE:

A Guide for Listening and Inner Healing Prayer: Meeting God in the Broken Places by Rusty Rustenbach (NavPress 2011) ISBN: 978-1-61747-086-8 – this book is recommended for a more in depth experience of Listening and Inner Healing Prayer.

The Word is Life

LESSON #1

HOMEWORK

God speaks to us today through his written Word, which has the amazing power to transform your life if you read and study it daily. It is living and powerful and discerns the thoughts and intents of our hearts (Hebrews 4:12-13). It is inspired by God and equips us for the work God has for our lives (2 Timothy 3:16-17). There are numerous Scriptures in the Bible where God tells us about the power of His Word to transform our lives:

Joshua 1:8 - *This Book of the Law shall not depart from your mouth, but you shall meditate in it day and night, that you may observe to do according to all that is written in it. For then you will make your way prosperous, and then you will have good success.*

Jeremiah 23:29 - *"Is not My word like a fire?" says the Lord, "And like a hammer that breaks the rock in pieces?"*

1 Peter 1:23 - *...the word of God ... lives and abides forever.*

1 Thessalonians 2:13 - *For this reason we also thank God without ceasing, because when you received the word of God which you heard from us, you welcomed it not as the word of men, but as it is in truth, the word of God, which also effectively works in you who believe.*

John 17:17 - *Sanctify them by Your truth. Your word is truth.*

Acts 20:32 - *So now, brethren, I commend you to God and to the word of His grace, which is able to build you up and give you an inheritance among all those who are sanctified.*

God's Word makes us prosperous and successful; it breaks up sin in our lives; it lives and abides forever; effectively works in our lives; brings truth; builds us up and gives an eternal inheritance. What awesome power and amazing promises!

We will be walking a journey together through the Word of God to learn how He transforms lives and brings hope and healing to His children who desire to know Him more. God loves you and He demonstrates His love all throughout the Bible, which is His written word of hope for all people. Let's begin our journey together and see what He has in store for you.

This Week's Memory Verse

Psalm 1:2-3 (NKJV) *"But his delight is in the law of the Lord, and in His law he meditates day and night. He shall be like a tree planted by the rivers of water that brings forth its fruit in its season, whose leaf also shall not wither; and whatever he does shall prosper."*

DAY 1

Read Psalm 1:1-6 and answer the following questions:

1. What is the law of the Lord?

___

2. If I meditate on the law of the Lord, what am I promised?

___

3. What happens if I don't meditate on the law of the Lord?

___

Practice writing your memory verse (Psalm 1:2-3).

DAY 2

Read Psalm 1:1-6 *out loud* and answer the following questions:

1. What did you notice about this passage that you did not notice yesterday?

___

2. Which verse jumps out at you the most? Why?

___

3. What would you like to say to God about what you observed in this passage today?

___

Practice writing your memory verse (Psalm 1:2-3).

DAY 3

Read Psalm 1:1-6 several times – *personalizing the passage* **by replacing 'the man' with [your name]; 'his' with 'my; and 'he' with 'I' for example. Then answer the following questions.**

1. What is God saying to me?

   _____

   _____

   _____

2. What would you like to say to God in return?

   _____

   _____

   _____

3. How do you think your life would change if you were to apply this Word to your life?

   _____

   _____

   _____

   Practice writing your memory verse (Psalm 1:2-3)

DAY 4

Sing Psalm 1:1-6 *to God while personalizing the Scripture* and answer the following questions:

1. How did you feel when you put a melody to the Word and sang this Scripture to Him?

___

2. What did God reveal to you when you sang this Scripture to Him that you did not notice before?

___

3. What value do you think there is in combining the Word with a melody?

___

Practice writing your memory verse (Psalm 1:2-3).

DAY 5

Try to recite Psalm 1:1-6 without looking at the passage. Then read the passage and answer the following questions:

1. Were you able to recite much of the passage from memory? Why/why not?

   _____

   _____

   _____

2. What have you learned from this passage that you can apply to your life?

   _____

   _____

   _____

3. What practical steps will you commit to in order to apply this Word to your life?

   _____

   _____

   _____

   Practice writing your memory verse (Psalm 1:2-3)

   Notes/Questions to bring to the next Group Session:

The Word is Life

LESSON #1

CLASSROOM DISCUSSION

Bible Facts

1. The _____ _____ of the Bible (____ Old Testament and _____ New Testament) were written:

   • By more than _____ _____ inspired by _____

   • Over a period of approximately _____ years

The Power of God's Word to Transform Lives

2. Scripture is profitable for _____, _____, _____, and _____ in righteousness (2 Timothy 3:16-17)

3. The Word of God is _____ and _____ (Hebrews 4:12-13)

4. The Word of God is a _____ of the _____ and _____ of the heart. (Hebrews 4:12-13)

5. The Word will _____ your life if you _____ what you learn to your life. (James 1:21-25)

6. We are to be _____ of the Word and not _____ only (James 1:21-25)

Workbook — Lesson #1   15

NOTES

The Enemy's Lies vs. God's Truth

LESSON #2

HOMEWORK

God loves you. Did you hear me? God loves you. No matter what you have done in your life, no matter how bad you think you are, or how far you have strayed from God - He loves you. He loves you so much that He sent his only Son to die on a cross and take the punishment for your sins upon Himself so that you can be reconciled to God. John 3:16 says God so loved the world that He gave His only begotten Son that whoever believes in Him should not perish but have everlasting life. That is Great News! God not only loves you – He knows every tiny detail about you because He created you just the way you are.

There is an enemy in this world that is intent on separating us from God. Sin entered the world in the Garden of Eden – when Satan tempted Adam and Eve to rebel against God by doing the one thing that God instructed Adam not to do - and they failed the test. (Read Genesis 2 & 3). At that time, sin entered into the world, and as a result we were all born sinners (Romans 3:10; 3:23).

Satan has been trying to destroy you since you were born. The Bible says that your enemy, the devil, prowls around like a roaring lion seeking someone to destroy (1 Peter 5:8). He is also referred to as the thief who comes to steal, kill and destroy (John 10:10). All of the negative things people have said to you or about you over the years were messages from the one who did not want to see you reconciled to God. People who said you were not good enough, that you would never amount to anything, and that you don't belong - were used as instruments by Satan to discourage you and separate you from God's truth about you.

The Bible says, just like Jeremiah, you were known by God before He formed you in your mother's womb (Jeremiah 1:5). He has a plan and a purpose for your life. In order to walk in your destiny, you need to see yourself like God sees you; truly understand your worth and refuse to listen to the voice of the enemy of your soul from this day forward.

Let God begin to show you His truth about your worth this week. As you read and study His Word and allow Him to speak to your heart, jot down what He wants you to apply to your life so you can share these jewels with your classmates next week.

This Week's Memory Verse:

Psalm 139:23-24 (NKJV) *"Search me, O God, and know my heart; try me, and know my anxieties; and see if there is any wicked way in me, and lead me in the way everlasting."*

DAY 1

Read Psalm 139 three times (once before answering each question) and answer the following questions:

1. What is Psalm 139 revealing about how much God cares for you?

___

2. What does it mean to be 'hedged' behind and before?

___

3. What would be different about my life if I truly believed every word in this passage of Scripture?

___

Practice writing your memory verse (Psalm 139:23-24).

DAY 2

Read Psalm 139 *out loud* and answer the following questions:

1. What did you notice about this passage that you did not notice yesterday?

___

2. Which verse jumps out at you the most? Why?

___

3. What would you like to say to God about what you observed in this passage today?

___

Practice writing your memory verse (Psalm 139:23-24).

DAY 3

1. What words immediately come to mind when you think about how you describe yourself? Write 10 words in the spaces below that describe how you feel about yourself (be honest).

   _____   _____

   _____   _____

   _____   _____

   _____   _____

   _____   _____

2. Which ones do you consider negative? Why?

   _____

   _____

   _____

   _____

3. Which ones do you consider positive? Why?

   _____

   _____

   _____

   _____

4. Do the 10 words you listed describe what you feel other people would say about you? Why/why not?

   _____

   _____

   _____

   _____

Read Psalm 139.

5. What does God say about you that is different from what you wrote above?

___

6. Whose 'voice' have you been listening to the most regarding your worth? Why do you think that is?

___

Practice writing your memory verse (Psalm 139:23-24).

DAY 4

Read Psalm 139 and answer the following questions:

1. How do you feel about asking God to search you and to know your heart? Is this comfortable for you? Why/why not?

_____

_____

_____

_____

_____

2. What has God revealed to you about your heart?

_____

_____

_____

_____

_____

3. What do you want to say to God about what He has been revealing to you this week?

_____

_____

_____

_____

Practice writing your memory verse (Psalm 139:23-24).

DAY 5

Read Psalm 139 and answer the following questions:

1. How does Psalm 139:11-12 apply to areas of sin in your life?

2. How does Psalm 139:13-16 address the issue of sin?

3. What practical steps will you commit to in order to apply this Word to your life?

Practice writing your memory verse (Psalm 139:23-24).

The Enemy's Lies vs. God's Truth

LESSON #2

CLASSROOM DISCUSSION

The Enemy Has Been Trying to Destroy You

1. Your _____, the devil, walks about like a _____ _____ seeking someone to devour. (1 Peter 5:8)

2. Our _____ is the _____ of the brethren, who stands before _____ day and night pointing out what we have done wrong. (Rev 12:10)

3. The _____ desires to _____ us as _____, but Jesus _____ for us that our _____ may not fail. (Luke 22:31)

God Loves You

4. Before God _____ you in your mother's womb, He _____ you, and He _____ you. (Jeremiah 1:5, and Psalm 139:13)

5. _____ things work together for _____ to those who _____ _____ and are _____ _____ according to His _____. For those He _____ He also _____ to be conformed to the _____ of Jesus. (Romans 8:28-29)

6. _____ knows the _____ He thinks towards you, thoughts of _____ and not _____ – to give you a _____ and a _____. (Jeremiah 29:11)

You are to be _____ with might through _____ _____ in the _____ man, that _____ may dwell in your heart through _____, being _____ and _____ in love you may be able to comprehend what is the _____ and _____ and _____ and _____ – to _____ the love of _____. (Eph 3:16-19)

NOTES

Freedom in Truth

LESSON #3

HOMEWORK

Jesus forgives, rescues, sets free and heals when we bring our brokenness to him. The Bible says that when we confess our sins, He is faithful and just to forgive us of our sins and to cleanse us from all unrighteousness (1 John 1:9).

There are numerous instances in the Bible where people called out or reached out to Jesus in their brokenness and asked Him for help, and He never turned them away. (Matthew 9:27-29; Mark 1:40-41; Luke 8:43-48; Matthew 20:29-34; Matthew 14:22-31). There are also instances where Jesus initiated the contact with a hurting person and healed them (John 5:1-9; Luke 13:10-13; John 4:1-26, 28). Finally, there are instances where others assisted another person to get to Jesus for healing, or they came to Him for healing on behalf of someone else (Luke 5:17-26; John 4:46-54).

In addition to those who sought healing from Jesus, there were people (even religious leaders) who exposed other's sins for the sake of public humiliation, as well as trying to trap Jesus in His response so they could justify killing Him (John 8:1-11). Other times, they did not physically expose the sinner but harbored ill will towards them in their hearts, and Jesus consistently responded to the sinner with mercy, grace, and forgiveness (Luke 7:36-50). The Bible also reveals that some people are afflicted with infirmities, not because of sin in their lives, but because God desires to use their lives and their testimony to reveal His glory. The story of the man who was blind from birth is one such example (John 9:1-11).

When others condemn you for what they see in your life, or you condemn yourself for your behavior, know that God is standing by to forgive you and cleanse you from all unrighteousness. He is waiting for you to expose your shortcomings to the light, to confess your sins to Him and allow Him to set you free so he can begin to heal your pain.

God's Word is truth, and if you abide in His Word, He will show you the truth about who He is, and how much He loves you. The truth He wants you to understand and incorporate into every aspect of your being will transform your life forever!

This Week's Memory Verse

John 8:31-32 (NKJV) *Then Jesus said to those Jews who believed Him, "If you abide in My word, you are My disciples indeed. And you shall know the truth, and the truth shall make you free."*

DAY 1

Read John Chapter 8 and answer the following questions:

1. What is Jesus revealing to the Pharisees (and to us) about Himself in this chapter?

_____
_____
_____
_____
_____
_____

2. Re-read John 8:1-11. How did Jesus respond to the scribes and Pharisees who brought the woman to Jesus?

_____
_____
_____
_____
_____
_____

3. How did Jesus respond to the woman? What did He say to her?

_____
_____
_____
_____
_____
_____

4. Based on this passage of Scripture, if Satan (the enemy of your soul) were to drag you in front of Jesus to accuse you of your sins publicly, how do you think Jesus will respond to you?

_____

_____

_____

_____

5. How does that make you feel? Are you comforted or fearful? Why?

_____

_____

_____

_____

_____

_____

Practice writing your memory verse (John 8:31-32).

DAY 2

Read John Chapter 8 and answer the following question:

1. What did you notice today in this chapter that you missed when you read the passage yesterday?

2. Re-read John 8:12-20. What does Jesus mean when He says He is the 'light of the world'? What does that mean to you personally?

3. What does Jesus mean when He says that the Pharisees judge according to the 'flesh' (verse 15)? How does this relate to John 8:1-11?

4. Have you judged yourself according to the 'flesh' like the Pharisees? If so, what do you think Jesus is telling you in this passage of Scripture?

_____

_____

_____

_____

_____

_____

_____

_____

_____

_____

Practice writing your memory verse (John 8:31-32).

DAY 3

Read John 3:1-21 and answer the following questions:

1. How does this passage of Scripture directly relate to John 8:1-11?

2. What does Jesus reveal to us in John 3:1-21 about salvation?

3. Are you saved? Have you been 'born again' (of Spirit)? How do you know?

4. What do you notice in John 3:1-21 and in John 8:12-20 about 'light' and 'darkness'?

_____

_____

_____

_____

_____

_____

_____

_____

_____

_____

Practice writing your memory verse (John 8:31-32).

DAY 4

Read John Chapter 8 and answer the following questions:

1. What verse or verses are speaking to your heart? Why?

_____
_____
_____
_____
_____
_____
_____
_____

2. Re-read John 8:21-32. Jesus is saying to the Pharisees (and to us) that we will die in our sins if we do not believe what? What is He talking about in verses 21-27?

_____
_____
_____
_____
_____
_____

3. What does it mean to 'abide' in God's Word? If you abide in His Word, what does that make you (v.31)?

_____
_____
_____
_____
_____

4. If we abide in His Word and are disciples of Jesus Christ, what does He promise in verse 32? What does that mean to you personally?

_____

_____

_____

_____

_____

_____

_____

_____

_____

_____

_____

_____

Practice writing your memory verse (John 8:31-32).

DAY 5

Read John Chapter 8 and answer the following questions:

1. What verse or verses are speaking to your heart? Why?

2. Re-read John 8:33-59. In what areas of your life have you been in 'bondage to sin'? Be specific. We all have multiple areas of sin in our lives. How has this bondage affected you?

3. What does Jesus say about the devil (Satan) in verse 44 that we learned last week in other Scripture passages?

4. What does Jesus say in verse 36 that you can apply to your life?

5. What would it 'look like' and 'feel like' if you were truly free from the sins that have you in bondage? Be specific.

6. What practical steps will you commit to in order to apply this Word to your life?

Practice writing your memory verse (John 8:31-32).

Notes/Questions to bring to the next Group Session:

Freedom in Truth

LESSON #3

CLASSROOM DISCUSSION

1. Jesus does not _____ sinners – He _____ them. (John 8:1-11)

2. When we encounter Jesus and our _____ are exposed to Him – he _____ our _____ and tells us to go and _____ _____ _____. (John 8:11)

3. If we _____ our _____ He is faithful and just to _____ us our _____ and _____ us from all _____. (1 John 1:9)

4. Jesus reacts to our _____ with _____ and _____. (Luke 7:44-50)

5. _____ in Jesus is what saves us and gives us _____. (Luke 7:50)

Testimony Sharing

- When did you first experience a life-controlling issue that you are not proud of (how old were you)?
- What do you think is the cause of your behavior?

NOTES

Hearing God's Voice

LESSON #4

HOMEWORK

God first spoke to man shortly after He created the first human beings. (Genesis 1:26-28). All throughout the Bible, we see instances where God spoke to people in various ways through:

- His Audible voice - Adam and Eve - Genesis 3; Samuel - 1 Samuel 3; Moses - Exodus 3; Abraham – Genesis 12; Elijah – 1 Kings 19:11-13; Gideon – Judges 6
- His Prophets – Samuel to Saul – 1 Samuel 15; Nathan to David – 2 Samuel 12; Jonah to the people of Nineveh – Jonah 3
- His Written Word – King Josiah – 2 Kings 22; People of Jerusalem - Nehemiah 8:1-11

When Jesus walked this earth in human form, He communicated directly with humanity through His teachings and interactions with people. In the book of John, Jesus reveals that He is the Good Shepherd and that His sheep know His voice (John 10:1-27). Jesus was saying, like sheep who know the voice of their shepherd (protector, provider, comforter), those who know Him as Lord and Savior know His voice.

As Jesus was nearing the end of His time on this earth, He promised that He would send the Holy Spirit to be with us and to speak to us after He departed this earth (John 14:25-26; John 16:12-15; Hebrews 10:15-16; 1 Corinthians 2:9-12). The Holy Spirit speaks to us today through promptings in our spirit.

God has been speaking to mankind in various ways ever since He created us, and the Bible tells us that He is the same yesterday, today, and forever (Hebrews 13:8). Therefore, we can be sure that He is speaking to you and me today. We just need to be still and learn to listen and know His voice.

When learning to hear the voice of God, keep in mind His character. God will never contradict His character when communicating with you. We know the character of God by studying His Word. You will know how God will react to circumstances and situations in your life by reading about how He has reacted to similar situations in the Bible.

This Week's Memory Verse

1 Corinthians 2:12 (NKJV) *Now we have received, not the spirit of the world, but the Spirit who is from God, that we might know the things that have been freely given to us by God.*

DAY 1

Read John Chapter 10:1-30 and answer the following questions:

1. What is Jesus revealing about Himself when He refers to Himself as the Good Shepherd?

_____

_____

_____

_____

_____

2. Why is it important for a flock of sheep to know the voice of their shepherd? How does this relate to you and your Shepherd (Jesus)?

_____

_____

_____

_____

3. How have you experienced 'hearing' the voice of God in your life? How did you know it was God's voice?

_____

_____

_____

_____

_____

4. If you have never repented of your sins, asked God for forgiveness, and accepted Jesus as your personal Lord and Savior, you will not be able to hear God's voice. John 8:47 says that people who are of God hear His voice. If you have never taken this bold step and turned your life over to Jesus, you will not be able to hear God's voice and obtain the healing and deliverance you are seeking.

If you have never accepted Jesus as your personal Lord and Savior, you can do it right now and change your eternal destiny. All that is required is that you pray to God:

A) Acknowledging that you are a sinner (Romans 3:10, 3:23)

B) Believing that Jesus died on the cross for the forgiveness of your sins, was buried and rose again where He is now at the right hand of the Father. Ask Jesus to forgive your sins (Romans 5:12, 5:8)

C) Accepting the free gift of Salvation that Jesus is extending to you (Romans 6:23, 10:9-10)

If you just accepted Jesus for the first time, contact your Facilitator or Accountability Partner right away so they can celebrate with you! Know also that the angels in heaven are rejoicing over your decision (Luke 15:10). You will now begin to hear the voice of God, and He will begin to direct your life.

Practice writing your memory verse (1 Corinthians 2:12).

DAY 2

Read 1 Samuel Chapter 3 and answer the following questions:

1. Why do you suppose Samuel did not recognize the voice of God when he heard it?

2. What do you notice about the time of day and circumstances of God's speaking to Samuel?

3. What do you notice about God's persistence with communicating to Samuel? Does this encourage or discourage you? Why?

4. How did Samuel react to the information that God communicated with him? What did He do when Eli questioned him?

_____

_____

_____

_____

_____

_____

5. Do you think God has been trying to communicate with you? What is He saying and how have you responded?

_____

_____

_____

_____

_____

_____

_____

Practice writing your memory verse (1 Corinthians 2:12).

DAY 3

Read 1 Kings 18:20 – 19:18 and answer the following questions:

1. How do you think that Elijah could go from the mountain top experience of seeing the magnificent power of God demonstrated through him to valley of depression and fear for his life in so short a time? Has this ever happened to you? How did you respond?

___

2. What was communicated by God to Elijah in 1 Kings 19:5-8, and how was it communicated to him?

___

3. What was communicated to Elijah in 1 Kings 19:9? Why do you think this question was asked of Elijah?

___

4. What was revealed to Elijah about the how God communicates with us in 1 Kings 19:11-12? How did Elijah respond to the voice of God?

___

5. What is this passage of Scripture teaching you about how God will speak to you? What might you have to do to hear His voice?

___

Practice writing your memory verse (1 Corinthians 2:12).

DAY 4

Read Romans 8:1-17 and answer the following questions:

1. What verse or verses are speaking to your heart about how God communicates with you? How you can 'hear' His voice? Why?

2. What does Romans 8:5-7 say about being spiritually-minded? What do you think this means for you with respect to hearing God's voice?

3. Do you think there is anything in your life that is hindering you from hearing God's voice? If so, what do you need to do to 'clear the channel' with God so you can hear His voice clearly?

_____

_____

_____

_____

_____

_____

_____

Practice writing your memory verse (1 Corinthians 2:12).

DAY 5

Read 1 Corinthians 2:1-16 and answer the following questions:

1. What verse or verses are speaking to your heart? Why?

_____

_____

_____

_____

_____

_____

2. What is Paul saying in 1 Corinthians 2:10-13 about the Holy Spirit and how He communicates with us/speaks to us?

_____

_____

_____

_____

_____

_____

3. What does Paul say about the natural man and his understanding of the things of God in verse 14? What does this mean for the unbeliever?

_____

_____

_____

_____

_____

4. When the Scripture says that we have the mind of Christ in verse 16, what does this mean with respect to our ability to discern the voice of God?

_____

_____

_____

_____

5. Did you learn something new about how to hear the voice of God in the lessons this week? If so, what?

_____

_____

_____

_____

6. What practical things will you commit to do in order to hear the voice of God and apply the Scriptures that you studied this week to your life?

_____

_____

_____

_____

Practice writing your memory verse (1 Corinthians 2:12).

Notes/Questions to bring to the next Group Session:

Hearing God's Voice

LESSON #4

CLASSROOM DISCUSSION

God 'speaks' to His children in a variety of ways:

1. God _____ to us through _____. (Romans 1:19-20)

2. God _____ to us through the _____ _____. (Romans 10:14; 1 Corinthians 1:21; Acts 10:42).

3. God _____ to us through _____ and _____. (Exodus 4:1-9; Acts 4:22; Acts 5:12; Hebrews 2:1-4).

4. God _____ to us when we _____ Him. (John 4:24; James 4:6; Acts 17:24-25).

5. God _____ to us through _____. (Acts 16:16-34).

6. God _____ to us through his _____. (1 Tim 3:16; James 1:21-25).

NOTES

Prayer – Communicating with God

LESSON #5

HOMEWORK

Prayer is one of the ways we communicate with God. We have already studied how God communicates with us. Now, we will focus on one of the ways we can communicate with God. As hard as it may be to comprehend, God really wants to hear from you. In fact, the Bible says that we are to pray without ceasing (1Thessalonians 5:17). By this, we are to always be in a posture of prayer – talking to God and listening to Him.

There are no special requirements for prayer. Some people are unsure and even fearful about prayer because they have never been taught how to pray, or they have not spent time with others who are comfortable with prayer to learn from them. Some people think that God requires a special formula or eloquent words to be spoken before He will listen and respond. Nothing could be farther from the truth! If you don't believe me, let's look at some prayers in the Bible that were not lengthy or eloquent and were still answered by God:

- "Lord, save me!" (Matthew 14:30)
- "Now Hannah spoke in her heart; only her lips moved, but her voice was not heard..." (1 Samuel 1:13)
- "Jesus, Son of David, have mercy on me!" (Luke 18:38)
- "Therefore, give to Your servant an understanding heart to judge Your people, that I may discern between good and evil. For who is able to judge this great people of Yours?" (1 Kings 3:9)

God wants to hear from you. Prayer is a means to develop an intimate relationship with Him. Just like you spend time talking to your friends about everything in your life, talking to God about those same things is prayer. The Bible tells us that if we develop intimacy with Him and know His Word, our wills becomes aligned with the will of God and we can ask for whatever we want and it will be given to us (John 15:7).

Even when we don't know what to pray for or how to pray, God has already given every born-again Christian His Holy Spirit who makes intercession for us in accordance with the will of God (Romans 8:26-27). That is great news! God even gives us what we need to communicate with Him in prayer. If you don't already have a regular prayer life, begin right now and your life will never be the same!

This Week's Memory Verse:

<u>1 John 5:14-15</u> (NKJV) *14Now this is the confidence that we have in Him, that if we ask anything according to His will, He hears us. 15And if we know that He hears us, whatever we ask, we know that we have the petitions that we have asked of Him.*

DAY 1

Read Matthew 6:5-13 and answer the following questions:

1. What is Jesus revealing to us about how we should pray? (v.9-13). Notice how the focus of the prayer begins on God before the first request is made of Him.

   _____
   _____
   _____
   _____
   _____
   _____

2. What does Jesus think about those who pray eloquent prayers full of vain repetitions? (v.5-8).

   _____
   _____
   _____
   _____
   _____

3. In verse 8, Jesus says that God already knows the things we have need of. Why do you suppose He wants us to pray if He already knows what we need?

   _____
   _____
   _____
   _____
   _____
   _____

4. What do you notice about the model prayer in verse12? What is Jesus saying here?

_____

_____

_____

_____

_____

_____

_____

_____

5. Do you feel uncomfortable praying? Why/why not?

_____

_____

_____

_____

_____

_____

_____

Practice writing your memory verse (1 John 5:14-15).

DAY 2

Read Nehemiah 1:1-2:8 and answer the following questions:

1. What can you say about Nehemiah's heart and his posture towards God when you read his prayer? (Nehemiah 1:5-11)

2. What do you notice about Nehemiah's prayer in Chapter 1 verses 8-10? What is Nehemiah saying to God in these verses?

3. How did God move on behalf of Nehemiah's prayer (review Nehemiah 2:1-4)? Do you believe God still makes things happen in response to our prayers? Why/why not?

_____

_____

_____

_____

_____

_____

_____

_____

_____

_____

4. What did Nehemiah do even though he was afraid when the king noticed his downcast face and questioned him? (Nehemiah 2:2-5) What was the result?

_____

_____

_____

_____

_____

_____

_____

_____

_____

_____

5. Have you ever prayed and seen God do miraculous things as a result? If you have not personally experienced this yet, has this happened to someone you know? Briefly describe:

Practice writing your memory verse (1 John 5:14-15).

DAY 3

Read Psalm 51 and answer the following questions:

1. This Psalm was written by King David in repentance for the sins he committed against Bathsheba and Uriah (2 Samuel Chapters 11 and 12). How does David begin his prayer in verses 1-3?

_____

_____

_____

_____

2. Knowing what you know about the story from 2 Samuel Chapters 11 and 12, what do you notice in verse 4? Why did David say this to God?

_____

_____

_____

_____

3. What is David asking God to do for him in verses 7-15?

_____

_____

_____

_____

4. What is David revealing to us about what our posture should be when we pray to God in verses 16-17?

5. Read Acts 13:22 and Hebrews 11:32-34. Are you encouraged by the fact that God still loved and honored David even though he sinned? Explain.

Practice writing your memory verse (1 John 5:14-15).

DAY 4

Read Judges 6:11-40 and answer the following questions:

1. What did Gideon say in response to God's charge to defeat the Midianites? (v.14-15). Have you ever expressed your inadequacy to God in response to something that God has asked you to do? Explain.

2. What did Gideon do after God reassured him that He would be with him and that Gideon would indeed defeat the Midianites? (v.17). Did God answer that prayer? (v.18-21). How?

3. What did you notice about Gideon's walk of faith as he begins to do what God is asking him to do in verses 25-35?

_____

_____

_____

_____

_____

_____

4. Do you think God is upset with Gideon when he continues to ask for signs in verses 36-40? Why/why not?

_____

_____

_____

_____

_____

_____

Practice writing your memory verse (1 John 5:14-15).

DAY 5

Read 2 Kings 19:8-37 and answer the following questions:

1. What did King Hezekiah do in response to the threat that was directed towards him? (v. 10-19). Have you responded similarly to threats directed at you? Explain.

2. What was God's response to Hezekiah's prayer? (v.20, 35, 37). Why do you think God responded the way He did?

3. If you immediately took every concern you have to God, instead of exhausting all of your other resources first (friends, family members, professionals, etc.), do you think God would respond to you like he did to Hezekiah? Why/why not?

4. What are some of the things you have learned about prayer this week?

5. What will you commit to apply to your life from this week's lesson?

6. Do you currently have a prayer partner? If not, begin thinking about at least one person you would consider to begin praying with on a regular basis and write their name in the blank below.

Practice writing your memory verse (1 John 5:14-15).

Notes/Questions to bring to the next Group Session:

Prayer – Communicating with God

LESSON #5

CLASSROOM DISCUSSION

Our Prayers Move God on our Behalf

1. God will _____ His _____ towards us when we pray. (Psalm 116:2; Psalm 17:6; Psalm 10:17; 1 Peter 3:12)

2. God will sometimes _____ our prayers before we _____ _____. (Isaiah 65:24)

3. God _____ the prayers of the _____. (Psalm 22:24; Jonah 2:2,7)

4. When we _____ ourselves, and _____, and _____ from our _____ ways, God will _____ us. (2 Chronicles 7:14)

Power of Praying Scripture Back to God

5. You can be _____ that God will _____ what He has said in His _____. (Isaiah 55:11)

6. When God has _____ something specific in Scripture we can be _____ that _____ will answer that prayer. (Deuteronomy 30:2-5/Nehemiah 1:9)

Jesus Intercedes (Prays) on our Behalf

7. Jesus _____ for _____ believers to be _____ with Him. (John 17:20-26)

8. Jesus _____ on our behalf as our _____ _____ (Hebrews 7:25; 1 John 2:1)

9. _____ is at the _____ _____ of the Father _____ on our behalf. (Romans 8:34)

NOTES

Fall of Man Root Causes of Sin

LESSON #6

HOMEWORK

Many of us have heard and know the story of Adam and Eve in the Garden of Eden where the serpent (devil) tempted them to eat of the tree of the knowledge of good and evil, which God specifically prohibited them from eating (Genesis 2:1-17; 3:1-6). At that moment, sin entered into the world and has been passed down through all generations of man (Romans 3:10; 3:23). As a result of their sin, and to keep them from eating of the tree of life and remaining in sin forever, God banished Adam and Eve from the Garden (Genesis 3:22-24).

The remainder of the Bible is about God's marvelous plan for reconciling us to Himself through the sacrificial love of Jesus Christ, who died on the cross for our sins so we could be restored to God through justification and the free gift of righteousness (Rom 5:16-19). In the end, when all is said and done, all people who have accepted Jesus Christ as Lord and Savior and begin allowing God to transform their lives so they can live holy and pleasing to God, will be saved and will have access to the tree of life as God makes all things new (Romans 10:9; 10:23; Revelation 21:1-8; 22:1-5).

You and I were born into sin. So were our parents, our grandparents, our brothers and sisters, our teachers, our coaches, our pastors, our _____ – you name it, we were all born into sin. As you well know from your own life, sinners have a natural propensity to remain in the flesh and to sin. Therefore, people get hurt as a result of these sinful interactions with each other. Sometimes, people hurt other people on purpose, and at other times, it is not done with any kind of intent – it just happens.

This week, you will be working on your personal timeline (Timeline/Root Cause Exercise follows Week 6 Day 5 Homework in the Workbook) to begin to understand how the things that you have experienced over your lifetime, and your response to those things, has resulted in your life-controlling sin issues. Please be diligent about working on that exercise this week, as it will begin your healing process.

It is also vitally important that we remain (abide) in the Word of God every day (John 8:31-32) because that is how God reveals His truth to us and how He sets us free. Therefore, we will continue to have daily reading assignments for this week, but there will not be as many questions to answer so you can focus on your timeline.

This Week's Memory Verse

Romans 6:12 (NKJV) *12Therefore, do not let sin reign in your mortal body, that you should obey it in its lusts.*

DAY 1

Read Romans 5:12 – 6:14 and answer the following questions:

1. What is God revealing to you in Romans 5:15-19 about how Jesus' sacrificial love, demonstrated by His dying on the cross so you could be free from sin, frees you from life-controlling sinful behavior?

___

___

___

___

___

___

___

___

2. Pray and ask God to help you recall what you need to include as you work on your Timeline/Root Cause Exercise (behind Week 6 Day 5 Homework in this Workbook) so you can begin to see the triggers and patterns in your life that led to your bondage to sin.

    Practice writing your memory verse (Romans 6:12).

DAY 2

Read Romans 5:12 – 6:14 and answer the following questions:

1. What is God revealing to you in Romans 6:1-4 about how Jesus' sacrificial love, demonstrated by His dying on the cross so you could be free from sin, frees you from life-controlling sinful behavior?

_____

_____

_____

_____

_____

_____

_____

2. Pray and ask God to help you to recall what you need to include as you work on your Timeline/Root Cause Exercise so that you can begin to see the triggers and patterns in your bondage to sin.

   Practice writing your memory verse (Romans 6:12).

DAY 3

Read Romans 5:12 – 6:14 and answer the following questions:

1. What is God revealing to you in Romans 6:5-7 about how Jesus' sacrificial love, demonstrated by His dying on the cross so you could be free from sin, frees you from life-controlling sinful behavior?

   _____

   _____

   _____

   _____

   _____

   _____

   _____

   _____

2. Pray and ask God to help you recall what you need to include as you work on your Timeline/Root Cause Exercise so that you can find the triggers and patterns in your life that led to your bondage to sin.

   Practice writing your memory verse (Romans 6:12).

DAY 4

Read Romans 5:12 – 6:14 and answer the following questions:

1. What is God revealing to you in Romans 6:8-11 about how Jesus' sacrificial love, demonstrated by His dying on the cross so you could be free from sin, frees you from life-controlling sinful behavior?

_____

_____

_____

_____

_____

_____

_____

_____

2. Pray and ask God to help you to recall what you need to include as you work on your Timeline/Root Cause Exercise so that you can expose the triggers and patterns in your life that led to your bondage to sin.

   Practice writing your memory verse (Romans 6:12).

DAY 5

Read Romans 5:12 – 6:14 and answer the following questions:

1. What is God revealing to you in Romans 6:12-14 about how Jesus' sacrificial love, life-controlling sinful behavior?

_____

_____

_____

_____

_____

_____

_____

_____

2. Pray and ask God to help you recall what you need to include as you work on your Timeline/Root Cause Exercise so that you can expose the triggers and patterns in your life that led to your bondage to sin.

   Practice writing your memory verse (Romans 6:12).

   Notes/Questions to bring to the next Group Session:

TIMELINE/ROOT CAUSE EXERCISE

This exercise is for your eyes only. It will not be turned in to the facilitators. However, we will discuss the results of the exercise in class, and recommend that you share what you are learning about yourself with your Accountability Partner. Write what you feel comfortable writing – to help you remember for processing and discussion later.

You will be creating a timeline of your life from birth to now as if you were preparing to write your autobiography. The purpose of this exercise is to help you:

- Identify the significant things/events that have occurred in your lifetime (good and bad, joyful and painful) that cause you to think and behave the way you do;
- Recognize patterns of behavior in your life; and
- See how it all fits together to make you the person you have become (warts and all).

Add to your timeline as God continues to reveal things to you over the next several weeks.

Instructions for Completion

1. Pray and ask God to help you complete this exercise.

2. Work through each of the statements below and write down anything that comes to your mind.

3. Create a timeline of your life from your earliest memories and make notes along your timeline so you can see how some things that have occurred in your life may have contributed to your life-controlling issues, as well as patterns of behavior that you may not have been aware of before completing this exercise. Put your age next to significant milestones.

4. Write down what feelings you experienced at each major milestone on the timeline.

5. Pray and ask God to begin healing your heart for those past pains/disappointments.

6. Share some of what you are discovering about your life history and patterns with your Accountability Partner so they can pray for you more specifically.

Some Possible Root Causes of my life-controlling issues

1. Notes about my relationship with my mother and other significant women in my life from childhood until now.

___

2. Notes about my relationship with my father and other significant men in my life from childhood unti now.

___

3. Significant things that happened to me over my lifetime (both good and bad). Note your age at each milestone.

___

4. How I have felt about myself from childhood until now.

___

5. My history of drug/alcohol use (earliest exposure, and most recent).

___

___

___

___

6. Anything else God is revealing to me about my life.

___

___

___

___

Timeline – note this example is from the author's life and will likely be very different from your experiences)

For this exercise, you will use the next page to construct your own timeline.

Example

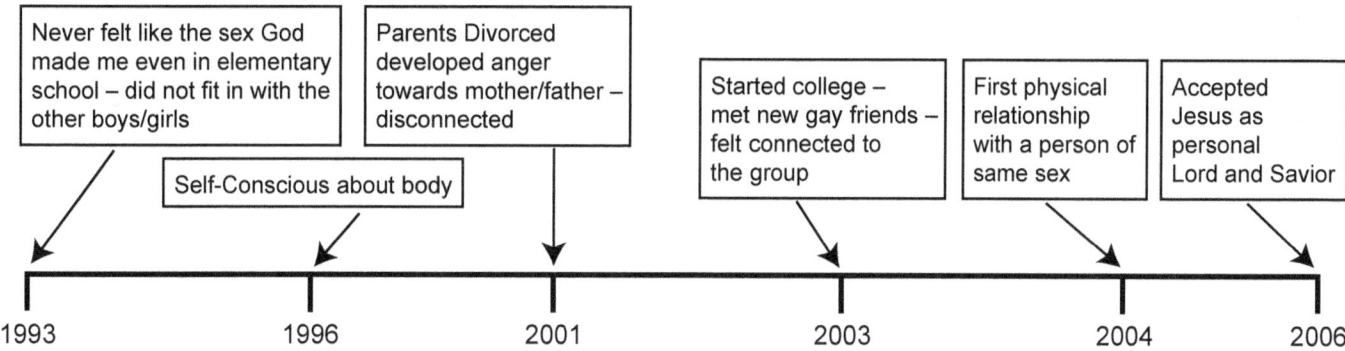

Feelings (example for a girl)

1993 *I never felt connected to other girls when I was young; I hung out with the boys and only played with them*

1996 *The kids in school made fun of me because I had a flat chest and didn't develop like the other girls. I felt embarrassed and ashamed about my body.*

2001 *When my parents divorced, I hated my mother because I felt that she didn't try to stay with dad. She wasn't there for me and I decided I didn't want to be like her.*

2003 *I met new friends in college that were gay; they were nice to me and accepted me for who I was. I finally felt like I belonged.*

2004 *My first sexual relationship with a woman was exhilarating. I felt like she really loved me and accepted me for who I am.*

2006 *Confused – want to line my life up with the Word of God but don't know how.*

TIMELINE/ROOT CAUSES AND MILESTONES

MAJOR MILESTONES AND FEELINGS

Fall of Man Root Causes of Sin

LESSON #6

CLASSROOM DISCUSSION

Abandonment

Genesis 21:8-16

Lies/Deceit and Trickery

Genesis Chapter 27

Sexual Abuse

2 Samuel Chapter 13

NOTES

Forgiveness

LESSON #7

HOMEWORK

Forgiveness is a gift we want from God when we sin against Him, but not one that we can easily give to people who hurt us. Most people find it very difficult to forgive someone who has hurt them, and they hold on to that hurt – going over and over it in their minds, sometimes for years. That hurt and pain becomes like a cancer inside. After reliving the incident which caused the pain for a period of time, they bury it deep inside and it festers below the surface causing damage to their physical health and well-being, not to mention their relationships with others. There are studies that suggest that holding on to un-forgiveness affects the immune system and can lead to chronic pain, heart disease, cancer, and other ailments.

God places a high value on forgiveness, an incredibly high value, demonstrated by the fact that he sent His Son Jesus to die on the cross for the forgiveness of your sins and mine. The Bible says, "for if you forgive men their trespasses, your heavenly Father will also forgive you. But if you do not forgive men their trespasses, neither will your Father forgive your trespasses." (Matthew 6:14-15).

God also gives us a timeframe in which to forgive when someone has hurt us. The Bible says, "Be angry, and do not sin: do not let the sun go down on your wrath, nor give place to the devil."(Ephesians 4:26-27). We are to forgive the trespasses of our offenders before the end of the day. Paul spoke to the Corinthians regarding forgiveness as follows, "now whom you forgive anything, I also forgive. For if indeed I have forgiven anything, I have forgiven that one for your sakes in the presence of Christ, lest Satan should take advantage of us; for we are not ignorant of his devices." (2 Corinthians 2:10-11). Don't you know that Satan loves unforgiveness? What better way to keep Christians in bondage to pain and suffering. What better way to keep us from forgiving those who have hurt us and prevent restoration of our relationships with one another?

Bishop T.D. Jakes says, "Forgiveness is a gift you give yourself," and he is right about that! Oftentimes, we hold on to unforgiveness for so long that the person who has hurt us has moved on with their lives, oblivious to the pain that we are still holding on to as a result of something they did, said, or failed to do or say. The unforgiveness hurts only the one who is holding on to it.

This week as you continue to work on your Timeline/Root Cause Exercise (Lesson #6), identify people who have hurt you in the past that you have never forgiven. As you work through the exercises this week, release your unforgiveness to God and let Him begin to heal your wounds that are a result of unforgiveness.

This Week's Memory Verse:

Ephesians 4:31-32 (NKJV) *31Let all bitterness, wrath, anger, clamor, and evil speaking be put away from you, with all malice. 32And be kind to one another, tenderhearted, forgiving one another, even as God in Christ forgave you.*

DAY 1

Read Matthew 6:9-15 and answer the following questions:

1. What is Jesus saying to you in this passage about forgiveness?

___

2. Why do you think Jesus says God will not forgive you if you refuse to forgive others?

___

3. Pray and ask God to reveal to you the names of people that you need to forgive, and write their names, along with a brief description of their offense towards you in the spaces below.

___

4. Continue to work on your Timeline/Root Cause Exercise (Lesson #6), adding details as God helps you to remember the things that you have experienced over your lifetime. As you are made aware of people that have hurt you, particularly those who you have not yet forgiven, write down their names along your timeline and ask God to help you to forgive them.

    Practice writing your memory verse (Ephesians 4:31-32).

DAY 2

Read Matthew 18:15-35 and answer the following questions:

1. What is Jesus revealing in verses 15-17 about the Biblical pattern for confronting a person who has offended you?

2. What does Jesus say about how often we should forgive those who hurt us?

3. In the parable of the servants in verses 23-35, Jesus shows us how wrong it is for us to treat each other like the wicked servant treated the one who owed him, after Jesus has forgiven us of so much! In the space below, write a prayer to God, asking for his forgiveness for your un-forgiveness towards others.

4. Continue to work on your Timeline/Root Cause Exercise (Lesson #6), adding details as God helps you to remember the things that you have experienced over your lifetime. As you are made aware of people that have hurt you, particularly those who you have not yet forgiven, write down their names along your timeline and ask God to help you to forgive them.

Practice writing your memory verse (Ephesians 4:31-32).

DAY 3

Read Matthew 5:21-26 and answer the following questions:

1. What is Jesus revealing to you in this passage of Scripture?

___

2. Why do you think that God wants you to be reconciled to someone who is upset with you before you offer your gift at the altar?

___

3. Who have you hurt that you need to ask for forgiveness? Write their name(s) and a brief description of what you did to hurt them below.

___

4. Continue to work on your Timeline/Root Cause Exercise (Lesson #6), adding details as God helps you to remember the things that you have experienced over your lifetime. As you are made aware of people that you have hurt, write down their names along your timeline and ask God for forgiveness.

Practice writing your memory verse (Ephesians 4:31-32).

DAY 4

Read Matthew 5:43-48 and answer the following questions:

1. What is Jesus saying to you in this passage of Scripture, as you think about the people that you have identified in your life that have hurt you?

   _____
   _____
   _____
   _____
   _____
   _____

2. Think about how much Jesus loved you even before you accepted Him as your Lord and Savior. What is He saying to you in this passage about unconditional love as it relates to forgiveness?

   _____
   _____
   _____
   _____
   _____

3. In the space below, write a prayer to God based on Matthew 5:43-48 focusing on one person that you have not yet forgiven for what they did to you.

   _____
   _____
   _____
   _____
   _____
   _____

4. Continue to work on your Timeline/Root Cause Exercise (Lesson #6), adding details as God helps you to remember the things that you have experienced over your lifetime. As you are made aware of people that have hurt you, particularly those who you have not yet forgiven, write down their names along your timeline and ask God to help you to forgive them.

Practice writing your memory verse (Ephesians 4:31-32).

DAY 5

Read Ephesians 4:17-32 and answer the following questions:

1. What is God revealing to you in this passage of Scripture about the power of forgiveness that you now have as a result of what Christ did for you?

   _____
   _____
   _____
   _____
   _____
   _____

2. What do verses 26-27 say about holding on to unforgiveness?

   _____
   _____
   _____
   _____

3. What do we do to God's Holy Spirit when we hold on to bitterness, wrath, anger, and unforgiveness? How do we avoid that in the future?

   _____
   _____
   _____
   _____
   _____
   _____

4. Continue to work on your Timeline/Root Cause Exercise (Lesson #6), adding details as God helps you to remember the things that you have experienced over your lifetime. As you are made aware of people that have hurt you, and people that you have hurt, particularly those who you have not yet forgiven, and those you still need to ask for forgiveness, write down their names along your timeline and ask God to help you to do what is right in His eyes.

Practice writing your memory verse (Ephesians 4:31-32). (add about 4-5 lines of space to practice memory verse)

Notes/Questions to bring to the next Group Session:

Forgiveness

LESSON #7

CLASSROOM DISCUSSION

What Forgiveness is and What it is Not

(Adapted from Resolving Everyday Conflict, Ken Sande & Kevin Johnson, (Baker Books 2011) © Peacemaker Ministries).

1. Forgiveness is NOT _____ (Isaiah 43:25)

2. Forgiveness is NOT _____ (Psalm 32:5)

What Forgiveness IS

3. Forgiveness IS a _____ _____ (Romans 5:8)

4. Forgiveness IS _____ and _____ be _____ (Romans 5:8)

5. Forgiveness IS an _____ _____ (Matthew 18:21-22)

There are Two Components of Forgiveness

6. The First Component of Forgiveness is the _____ Component (Romans 12:18)

7. The Second Component of Forgiveness is the _____ or _____ component. (Matthew 18:15)

Four Promises of Forgiveness

1. I will not _____ on this incident

2. I will not _____ this incident _____ and _____ it _____ you

3. I will not _____ to _____ about this incident

4. I will not allow this incident to _____ _____ us or _____ our personal relationship

Forgiveness

LESSON #7

IN-CLASS EXERCISE

Choose one person that you identified this week during your homework exercises that you have not yet forgiven for what they did or failed to do. Write their name here: _____

In the space below, write a letter to God expressing your "attitude of forgiveness" - your willingness to forgive that person regardless of whether they have asked for forgiveness or not, or even if they have passed away and are no longer alive. Completely release that person from the offense(s) in your letter to God. Be specific (these letters will not be shared with anyone unless you choose to share them).

_____

_____

_____

_____

_____

_____

_____

_____

_____

_____

_____

_____

_____

_____

After you express your complete forgiveness of that person, write a prayer of blessing over the life of the person who has offended you. Pray that God will bless them (Matthew 5:44). Also pray and ask God to heal your heart from the pain of the offense.

My prayer of blessing:

NOTES

Sexual Integrity

LESSON #8

HOMEWORK

What is sexual integrity? The definition of *integrity* is steadfast adherence to a strict moral or ethical code, the quality or condition of being whole or undivided (The American Heritage Dictionary of the English Language, 3rd Edition). Therefore, sexual integrity requires that we maintain a steadfast adherence to a strict moral or ethical code (biblical laws and principles) with respect to our sexual conduct. We have learned from the Word of God that there is absolutely n no sexual conduct that is authorized by God outside the confines of marriage between one man and one woman

We live in a highly sexually-charged society. You can't watch television, listen to the radio, pick up a magazine, or surf the Internet without being constantly bombarded with sexually charged stimulus. That is because we live in a fallen world raging from the effects of sin. People of the world follow after the lusts of the flesh and perpetuate this addiction through all forms of media. But we are called to be set apart from the world. God's will for us is our sanctification: that we should abstain from sexual immorality and know how to possess our bodies in sanctification and honor, not in passion of lust, like those who do not know God (1 Thessalonians 4:3-5)

You may be thinking this is easier said than done! And you are absolutely right. It is not easy, but we also have a promise from God: no temptation has overtaken you except such as is common to man; but God is faithful, who will not allow you to be tempted beyond what you are able, but with the temptation He will also make the way of escape, that you may be able to bear it (1 Corinthians 10:13).

In addition to studying Scriptures to help us in the area of sexual purity, we will also learn about some practical things we can do to diminish the raging desires of our carnal bodies that have been opened up and exposed to sexual impurity, until those desires fade over time. They will fade and no longer have the power to control you! Likewise, you also reckon yourselves to be dead indeed to sin, but alive to God in Christ Jesus our Lord. Therefore, do not let sin reign in your mortal body, that you should obey it in its lusts. And do not present your members as instruments of unrighteousness to sin, but present yourselves to God as being alive from the dead, and your members as instruments of righteousness to God. For sin shall not have dominion over you, for you are not under law but under grace (Romans 6:11-14).

God. For sin shall not have dominion over you, for you are not under law but under grace (Romans 6:11-14).

Even after we have removed the things that feed our sexual addictions, have disassociated ourselves from the people we used to sin sexually with, have stopped going to the places we used to go to that enabled us to sin, and we have done everything we know to do to put guards in place to protect us, we will still face temptations that will challenge us to revert back to our old habits. While you will not be protected from temptations that come your way, you must know that God will ALWAYS make a way of escape for you when you are faced with such temptations. 1 Corinthians 10:13 says, "No temptation has overtaken you except such as is common to man; but God is faithful, who will not allow you to be tempted beyond what you are able, but with the temptation will also make the way of escape, that you may be able to bear it." Isn't it incredible to know that God knows what you can bear? You may think that you are being tempted beyond what you can overcome, but God created you and knows you better than you know yourself. Look for the escape route that He has provided to you EVERY time you are tempted.

Furthermore, James 1:12 says, "Blessed is the man who endures temptation; for when he has been approved, he will receive the crown of life, which the Lord has promised to those who love Him." God encourages us to endure temptations when they arise. Endure means to bear with tolerance, or suffer patiently without yielding (The American Heritage Dictionary of the English Language). You CAN endure the temptations that come your way, and when you do, you will be rewarded. These temptations are temporary attempts by the enemy to get you to satisfy your flesh. When Satan is unsuccessful in his attempts to get you to revert back and dishonor God, he will leave. The word of God says, "Resist the devil and he will flee from you." (James 4:7) Resist the enemy of your soul and use the escape route that God has provided to you! Each time you endure the temptation and do not sin, you become stronger and stronger in the Lord.

This Week's Memory Verse:

1 Corinthians 6:18 (NKJV) *Flee sexual immorality. Every sin that a man does is outside the body, but he who commits sexual immorality sins against his own body.*

DAY 1

Read Romans 7:7 – 8:11 and answer the following questions:

1. What does this passage of Scripture say about sexual impurity?

_____
_____
_____
_____
_____
_____
_____
_____

2. Sexual impurity opens us up to the work of the enemy in our lives. Whenever we do something outside the will of God, we are guided into the hands of the enemy of our soul. Once we are exposed to sexual stimulation (outside of the confines of marriage between one man and one woman as prescribed in the Bible), it can lead to an addiction as strong as the 'high' in an addiction to drugs or alcohol. How has your sexual impurity opened you up to sexual addictions? How has this addiction controlled your life? Be specific.

_____
_____
_____
_____
_____
_____
_____
_____

3. Write a personal prayer to God about your sexual integrity. If you freely participated in sexual conduct outside of marriage, thereby violating sexual integrity, ask God for forgiveness. If someone violated you sexually, thereby opening you up to sexual sin, ask God to help you forgive that person or persons, and begin the healing process. In both cases, ask God to heal the deep wounds that you now have as a result of sexual sin and ask God to close the spiritual doors that have been opened in your life as a result of sexual sin and help you to maintain sexual purity from this day forward.

_____

_____

_____

_____

_____

_____

_____

_____

_____

Practice writing your memory verse (1 Corinthians 6:18).

DAY 2

Read 1 Thessalonians 4:1-8 and answer the following questions:

1. What does this passage say about sexual purity?

   _____
   _____
   _____
   _____
   _____

2. What does this passage say about God's will for you in the area of sexual purity, and how God views the person who continues to participate in sexual immorality?

   _____
   _____
   _____
   _____

3. What do these Scriptures (Ephesians 4:17-18 and Romans 6:19) say about what we need to do to abstain from sexual immorality?

   _____
   _____
   _____
   _____
   _____

4. What practical things will you do to maintain your sexual purity? What guards are you willing to put into place to help you overcome any temptation to go back to any former sexual addictions? Pray and ask God to reveal anything more in your home and life that you need to get rid of to help you overcome any sexual temptation.

___

___

___

___

___

___

Practice writing your memory verse (1 Corinthians 6:18).

DAY 3

Read 1 Corinthians 6:9-20 and answer the following questions:

1. What verse or verses in this passage are speaking to your heart? Why? Explain.

2. What do you notice about verses 11-14? What does this mean for you personally?

3. How does verse 12 relate to any level of sexual addictions that you may have in your life? What does Romans 8:12-14 say about the Power you have to overcome any temptation?

4. What does 1 Corinthians 6:18 say that you should do when tempted?

5. Read 1 Peter 5:8, 2 Corinthians 2:11, and James 4:7-8. How do these Scripture passages give us information and power to do what 1 Corinthians 6:18 commands us to do?

6. Do you struggle with compulsive sexual behaviors such as pornography viewing or compulsive masturbation? One way to get this under control is to identify the triggers in your life that lead you to act out in this way.

   H.A.L.T. is an acronym that stands for Hungry, Angry, Lonely, and Tired. It is often used in recovery circles. The items stand for the red flags to acting out. In other words, when you are lonely, you are most vulnerable to a fall. To prevent this, you need an action plan. The action plan can be both proactive/preventive and reactive/curative.

   The proactive/preventive plan helps you avoid getting lonely. A reactive/curative plan is when it's too late and loneliness has already peeked its evil head. You will then need to know what to do. In this exercise, you are asked to set up both a proactive/preventive and a reactive/curative plan using the H.A.L.T. acronym.

   When completing this exercise, think specifically about how these triggers (H.A.L.T.) habitually result in you 'rewarding' yourself or 'relieving' stress by acting out sexually, through viewing pornography and/or masturbating.

   I: **Proactive/preventive plan. What I will do to avoid the following from taking its toll:**

   <u>H</u>ungry –

   <u>A</u>ngry –

   <u>L</u>onely –

   <u>T</u>ired –

100   **ALL THINGS NEW** *A DISCIPLESHIP MINISTRY FOR LIFE TRANSFORMATION*

II: **Reactive/curative plan. What I will do when the following takes its toll:**

Hungry – _____

Angry – _____

Lonely – _____

Tired – _____

Planning ahead about how you will handle triggers that, in the past, regularly caused you to act out. It sets guards in place to help you in the future.

7. In the space below, write a prayer to God asking Him to help you in the areas of your life that you have identified above, to protect you from the temptations that, in the past, have controlled your life. You can start by personalizing the Lord's Prayer. (Matthew 6:9-13)

_____

_____

_____

_____

_____

_____

Practice writing your memory verse (1 Corinthians 6:18).

DAY 4

Read 1 Corinthians 10:1-13 and answer the following questions:

1. What does verse 8 say about the sexual immorality committed by the Israelites who were supposed to live holy lives, set apart for God, and His response to their sin (referring to Numbers 25:1-9)?

2. Do you think God has the same reaction to sexual sin today, or has He changed His mind over time? Why do you think He doesn't destroy Christians who actively participate in sexual immorality today? (See Hebrews 13:8, Romans 3:23, 2 Peter 3:9, and John 3:17.)

3. What warning are we given in 1 Corinthians 10:12? What practical things have you already established (or you need to establish) in your life to keep you from falling back into your old habits with respect to sexual immorality? Describe.

4. What does James 1:13-15 say about temptation?

_____

_____

_____

_____

_____

_____

_____

5. What does 1 Corinthians 10:13 say about the temptations that you will face to sin sexually? Can you think of examples from your life where God made a way for you to escape sexual temptation? Did you take the escape route or did you succumb to the temptation? Describe your experiences below.

_____

_____

_____

_____

_____

Practice writing your memory verse (1 Corinthians 6:18).

DAY 5

Read Titus 2:11-14 and answer the following questions:

1. What does this passage say about sexual immorality? How does this relate specifically to your life?

2. The grace of God brings salvation (Titus 2:11, see also Romans 5:15) and teaches us that we should deny ungodliness and worldly lusts and we should live soberly, righteously, and godly. In the space below, write a prayer to God thanking Him for His grace and affirming your commitment to embrace this verse of Scripture and apply it to your life.

3. Titus 2:14 says that Jesus will redeem us from every lawless deed and purify us. Read Ezekiel 37:23, Hebrews 9:14, and 1 John 1:7. What do these Scriptures reveal about the source of our purification/cleansing? Are you solely responsible for overcoming your sexual immorality or do you have help if you will submit to Christ's work in your life? Explain.

4. Have you ever been exposed to pornography? If yes, when were you first exposed to it, and what is the extent of your use of pornography?

_____

_____

_____

_____

_____

5. Pornography is readily available on the Internet, and is one of the most dangerous hooks to sexual addiction because it can be obtained so easily from the privacy of your home. If you are addicted to Internet pornography, there are tools available to help you to overcome this addiction.

   One tool is free accountability software (X3watch) that you can download to your computer to track your Internet usage, and send a report to your Accountability Partner so he/she can hold you accountable. You can also upgrade the software (X3watch Pro) for a nominal monthly fee, to additionally block your ability to access pornographic sites. If you struggle with addiction to Internet pornography, go to http://www.xxxchurch.com/ and investigate the X3watch software and other tools available on that web site. Another site with similar tools is available at http://www.covenanteyes.com/

6. Review the Sexual Integrity Resolution on the next page. We will be going over this in class. Are you ready to sign it?

_____

_____

_____

7. Take a fresh look at your Timeline/Root Cause Exercise (Lesson #6). Is there anything else God has revealed to you this week that you need to add to it?

_____

_____

Practice writing your memory verse (1 Corinthians 6:18).

Notes/Questions to bring to the next Group Session:

All Things New
Sexual Purity Resolution

Therefore, if anyone is in Christ, he is a new creation; things old have passed away; behold, all things have become new.
2 Corinthians 5:17

I do solemnly resolve, from this day forward, to maintain my sexual purity before God and man.
(John 8:34, Acts 24:16)

I refuse to be controlled by the lust of my flesh.
(1 John 2:16, Romans 13:14)

I vow to remove from my home and my life any and all things that tempt me to backslide into sexual impurity.
(2 Corinthians 7:1, 1 John 3:3)

I vow to take every thought captive to the obedience of Christ and keep my mind pure.
(2 Corinthians 10:5, Romans 8:6)

I vow to guard my eyes, avoiding all forms of pornography.
(Matthew 5:28, Luke 11:34)

I vow to guard my heart, keeping it pure for God.
(Proverbs 4:23, Matthew 5:8)

Signed: _____ Date: _____

Witnesses: _____

Sexual Integrity

LESSON #8

CLASSROOM DISCUSSION

Sexual Integrity and Sexual Impurity

1. _____ does not tempt us to sin, we are tempted by _____ when we are away by our own _____ and enticed. (James 1:13-14)

2. _____ , not _____ we are _____ to sin, God will make a way of escape for us. (1 Corinthians 10:13)

3. We sin against God _____, when we look _____ with our eyes at another person. (Matthew 5:27-28)

4. Every sin that a man does is outside the body, but he who commits _____ _____ sins against his own _____. (1 Corinthians 6:18)

5. Whoever _____ sin is a _____ to sin. (John 8:34)

6. We are constantly fighting an _____ _____ between our _____ and our _____. (Romans 7:23)

The Mind and the Heart

7. Cast down arguments and every _____ _____ that exalts itself against the knowledge of God, bringing every _____ into _____ to the _____ of Christ. (2 Corinthians 10:5)

8. To be _____ minded is _____, but to be _____ minded is _____ and peace. (Romans 8:6)

9. We must set our minds on things _____ not on things on the _____. (Colossians 3:2)

10. Guard your _____ by _____ on the _____ to protect yourself from sexual immorality. (Proverbs 4:23, Matthew 15:19, Psalm 119:11)

Final Thoughts

11. If we _____ our sins, His is faithful and just to _____ us our sins and to _____ us from all unrighteousness. (1 John 1:9)

NOTES

Spiritual Warfare

LESSON #9

HOMEWORK

Spiritual warfare is something every true Christian faces. In fact, the Word of God says that we should not be surprised when fiery trials come into our lives, as though something strange were happening to us (1 Peter 4:12). When you accept Jesus Christ as Lord of your life, walk away from the things of the world, and turn your attention and your life towards the things of God, you become a target for the enemy who wants you back under his dominion and control.

The Bible tells us that we are to be self-controlled and alert because the devil prowls around like a roaring lion seeking someone to devour (1 Peter 5:8). We must understand how the enemy operates so he cannot take advantage of us (2 Corinthians 2:11). Thankfully, the Bible gives us instructions on how to identify the works of the enemy and how to arm ourselves for spiritual battle. This week, we will study the armor of God, which provides spiritual protection when we face spiritual warfare. We will also study the battle plans of the enemy so we will understand how he operates so we can defeat him.

This Week's Memory Verse

<u>**2 Corinthians 10:3-5**</u> (NKJV) *³For though we walk in the flesh, we do not war according to the flesh. ⁴For the weapons of our warfare are not carnal but mighty in God for pulling down strongholds, ⁵casting down arguments and every high thing that exalts itself against the knowledge of God, bringing every thought into captivity to the obedience of Christ,*

DAY 1

Read Ephesians 6:10-20 and answer the following questions:

1. What do verses 10-11 say about where our power comes from and who our enemy is?

_____

_____

_____

_____

_____

_____

_____

2. What does verse 12 say, and what does this mean to you personally? Think about your life and write down instances where you know you have experienced spiritual warfare and how you responded to those attacks.

_____

_____

_____

_____

_____

_____

_____

3. When we purpose in our hearts to follow God and walk away from the things of the world, we become a threat to the enemy of our souls. When we were living in the world worshipping idols (money, sex, fame, jobs, possessions, another person, etc.) and we were satisfying every fleshy desire of our hearts, we were no threat to the enemy. But now that we are turning our hearts toward God and determining to no longer live the life we once lived, we become a target for the enemy to attack. And the enemy often uses people to attack us.

1 Peter 4:1-4 and 1 Peter 4:12-13 say that we no longer live in the lusts of the flesh, but for the will of God. We spent enough of our past life doing the worldly things: walking in lewdness, lusts, drunkenness,

revelries, drinking parties, and abominable idolatries. Our old friends think it is strange that we have walked away from that life and they now speak evil of us. God tells us in His Word that we should not be surprised that we are experiencing fiery trials and spiritual warfare as if something strange is happening to us. He says that we should rejoice when we are attacked for following Christ because we are blessed, the Spirit of God rests on us! Think about it: if we were still living in the world and doing the things we used to do, God's Glory could not rest on us because God is Holy and requires us to live a holy life.

Write a prayer of thanks to God – thanking Him because you are His child, and thanking Him that you have been found worthy to be attacked by the His enemy and yours. Pray that He will give you the strength to endure the spiritual warfare attacks and that you will come out the victor!

_____

_____

_____

_____

_____

_____

_____

Practice writing your memory verse (2 Corinthians 10:3-5).

DAY 2

Read Ephesians 6:10-20 and answer the following questions:

1. What does verse 13 say we are to do with the 'whole armor of God' and what is the purpose of the armor that is revealed in this verse? What do you think it means to 'stand' – what does this mean to you personally?

   _____
   _____
   _____
   _____
   _____
   _____
   _____
   _____
   _____

2. Now we will study the Armor of God. Verses 14-17 describe important pieces of the armor of a Roman Soldier that were designed to protect his body in warfare. Each piece of armor described in the Scripture has a spiritual purpose, just like the physical armor had a purpose in the physical world to protect the various parts of the soldier's body. Look at the picture below as you read the Scripture and write down what God reveals to you about each piece of armor. Focus on the spiritual aspect of the armor and how each piece protects you today when you put on the 'armor of God.'

   Belt of Truth – the Truth is the truth of God's Word. Notice that the belt is the central piece of armor that holds many of the other pieces of armor in place. How does this relate spiritually?

   _____
   _____
   _____
   _____
   _____

Breastplate of Righteousness – Righteousness refers to the 'right standing' we now have because of what Jesus did for us on Calvary, and has nothing to do with our own worthiness apart from Christ. What do you notice about the breastplate that applies to your life spiritually?

_____

_____

_____

_____

Shoes of the Preparation of the Gospel of Peace – The Gospel is the "Good News" that Jesus came to die for our sins and that when we accept Him as Lord and Savior, our sins are wiped clean and we have everlasting life with Him. What do you notice about the soldier's shoes that you can apply to your life spiritually?

_____

_____

_____

_____

Shield of Faith – Faith is the substance of things hoped for and the evidence of things not seen (Hebrews 11:1). Pay particular attention to what the shield of faith does for you in verse 16. How does this piece of armor relate to your life spiritually?

_____

_____

_____

Helmet of Salvation – Salvation brings wholeness and deliverance from your sinful past. Think about what the helmet protects in light of what we have been discussing over the past couple of weeks. What do you see about the helmet that protects you spiritually?

_____

_____

_____

Sword of the Spirit – The Scripture says the Sword of the Spirit is the Word of God. What kind of weapon is a sword? Is it used for aggression or defense (or both)? How does this weapon apply to your life spiritually?

_____

_____

_____

3. Write a personal prayer to God asking Him to continue to teach you about His armor, and to remind you to put on the whole armor of God each and every day to protect you from the spiritual warfare battles that you will encounter as a child of God.

_____

_____

_____

_____

Practice writing your memory verse (2 Corinthians 10:3-5).

DAY 3

Now that we have studied the armor of God and thought about how it protects us for spiritual battles, we need to learn some things about spiritual warfare. Ephesians 6:12 says, *"for we do not wrestle against flesh and blood, but against principalities, against powers, against the rulers of the darkness of this age, against spiritual hosts of wickedness in the heavenly places."* Satan is real, and his demons are real.

Regarding spiritual warfare, there is a hierarchy of rank in the demon realm. Just like an Army in the physical realm has rank and order, the same is true in the spiritual realm.

Oftentimes in Scripture, you can see 'principalities and powers' listed together (Ephesians 1:21, 3:10, 6:12; Colossians 1:16, 2:10, 2:15). Principalities and powers are the highest-ranking demons and have authority over nations and cities. You can find Scripture reference to "principalities" in Daniel chapter 10 where an unnamed angel comes to Daniel in response to his prayers. In verse 13, it is revealed that the angel was fighting with the "prince of the kingdom of Persia" (a "principality" demon) and the powerful angel, Michael (also mentioned in Daniel 10:21; and 12:1) came to help the unnamed angel in that battle, freeing him to come to Daniel.

"Power" demons are associated with idol worship and can bring entire cities under the authority of Satan thorough idolatry. In Scripture, we can see an example of this in Acts 14:8-18, when Paul healed a crippled man and the city, prompted by demonic forces that resided there, rose up to worship Paul and Barnabas as idols.

We are not to fear "principalities and powers" because the Word of God says, *"*[37]*yet in all these things we are more than conquerors through Him who loved us.* [38]*For I am persuaded that neither death nor life, nor angels nor principalities nor powers, nor things present nor things to come,* [39]*nor height nor depth, nor any other created thing, shall be able to separate us from the love of God which is in Christ Jesus our Lord."* (Romans 8:37-39)

1. Reflect on what you now know about principalities and powers. What does Romans 8:37-39 say about the effect that these demons will have on you if you encounter them?

_____

_____

_____

_____

_____

_____

2. How do you think putting on the armor of God protects you from demonic attacks? What particular pieces of the armor are most useful? Why?

_____

_____

_____

_____

_____

_____

3. Write a prayer to God asking Him to help you to discern when you are under spiritual attack, so you will know how to respond. Ephesians 6:12 reveals that we don't wrestle against flesh and blood (other people), but against demonic forces that use people to get to us. I don't know about you but oftentimes, when I encounter strong opposition and situations where it seems that certain people are 'out to get me,' the quicker I am able to recognize these attacks as spiritual and not physical, the sooner I begin to pray for strength to deal with the situation, and the sooner the attack passes. In the space below, ask God to increase your spiritual discernment and to teach you how to successfully fight the spiritual battles you will face.

_____

_____

_____

_____

_____

_____

Practice writing your memory verse (2 Corinthians 10:3-5).

DAY 4

Ephesians 6:12 says, *"for we do not wrestle against flesh and blood, but against principalities, against powers, against the rulers of the darkness of this age, against spiritual hosts of wickedness in the heavenly places."*

Yesterday, we learned about principalities and powers. Today, we will focus on the rulers of darkness. Rulers of darkness are the third tier of demons. We see an example of this demon in the story of the two demon-possessed men in the country of the Gergesenes (Matthew 8:28-34), and in the demon-possessed man of the Gadarenes (Mark 5:1-9; Luke 8:26-33). These demons rule in areas of darkness (in both cases, the demon-possessed men were living in the tombs).

1. Read Matthew 8:28-34. What does verse 29 reveal about the demon's recognition of Jesus and His power over them? (See James 2:19.) What are they concerned about? (See Matthew 25:41.)

2. What does Matthew 8:31-32 reveal about the ability of demons to act on their own?

3. Read Mark 5:1-19 and Luke 8:26-33. What more do we learn about this demon from the accounts in Mark and Luke?

_____

_____

_____

_____

_____

_____

4. Legion – refers to a major unit of a Roman army consisting of about six thousand men. Why do you think there was such a vicious attack on this one man? Have you ever felt like a legion of demons was attacking you? Why do you think that the enemy would send such great opposition your way? Read Mark 5:19-20 and Luke 8:39. Does this help you to understand why the enemy has targeted you?

_____

_____

_____

_____

_____

_____

Practice writing your memory verse (2 Corinthians 10:3-5).

DAY 5

Ephesians 6:12 says, *"for we do not wrestle against flesh and blood, but against principalities, against powers, against the rulers of the darkness of this age, against spiritual hosts of wickedness in the heavenly places."*

So far, we have learned about principalities and powers and rulers of darkness. Today, we will focus on the lowest-ranking demons - 'spiritual hosts of wickedness.' They target individuals and are named by what they do and how they manifest in a person's life: spirit of lust, pride, confusion, bitterness, doubt, perversion, addiction, adultery, fear, etc. They tempt man to sin by focusing attention on the carnal flesh.

1. Do you recognize any of these demons in your life? What do you think are the most effective pieces of your spiritual armor to combat these demons? Explain by naming each one that you recognize in your life and what you now know to do to combat that particular demon.

___

___

___

___

___

___

Demons gain entrance (a foothold) into our lives when we sin. Ephesians 4:26-27 says, *"²⁶Be angry, and do not sin": do not let the sun go down on your wrath, ²⁷nor give place to the devil."* A foothold is all that it takes for Satan to prop open the door to allow demonic activity into our lives to torment us and build strongholds that make it difficult to rid ourselves of these demons. When we sin, or when someone sins against us and we are unwilling to forgive, it is as if a 'home' has been created in us for the demon to live. Jesus describes this phenomenon in Luke.

2. Read Luke 11:14-26. What is Jesus saying in verses 14 and 21-26 that gives us insight to how determined demons are to make a 'home' in our lives?

___

___

___

___

3. Some examples of demonic 'homes' that advance to strongholds follow, including the 'root causes' for the establishment of this 'home.' These are only examples to demonstrate how demonic bondages occur in people's lives.

Bondage to Lust and Pornography – lust and pornography are *rooted* in lack of love. Lust and pornography are the *demonic home* that contains a nest of demons (lust, pornography, perversion, etc.)

Bondage to Rejection – prior rejection (especially at a young age and by someone close to you) creates a deep wound creating a fleshly bondage where the person feels worthless and worthy to be rejected, which builds a stronghold of self-hate, self-rejection, etc. which is a demonic home that contains a nest of demons (rejection, rebellion, self-hate, etc.)

Bondage to Bitterness – can be rooted in a deep wound that occurs, such as rape, molestation, incest, etc. whereby a person feels 'used' and thinks they cannot forgive, which affects their relationships with other people as well. This creates unforgiveness and hatred towards the abuser, which becomes a demonic home that contains a nest of demons (hate, anger, resentment, etc.)

Do any of these examples resonate with you? If so, which one(s) and how?

_____

_____

_____

_____

_____

_____

_____

_____

_____

_____

_____

4. Doors that openly invite demonic activity into our lives include such things as participating in witchcraft, the occult, astrology, horoscopes, séances, hypnotism, cursing, sexual sins, idolatry, drug and alcohol abuse, etc.

   In the space below, identify any activities in your life that you have participated in that have invited demonic spirits into your life. Then write a prayer to God asking for forgiveness for what you have identified and pray that the Lord will deliver you from all demonic spirits that are tormenting you, and pray that the Lord will close every door and permanently seal every door with the blood of Jesus Christ in the name of Jesus.

   _____

   _____

   _____

   _____

   _____

5. Take a fresh look at your Timeline/Root Cause Exercise (Lesson #6). Is there anything else God has revealed to you this week that you need to add to it?

   _____

   _____

   _____

   _____

   _____

   Practice writing your memory verse (2 Corinthians 10:3-5).

   Notes/Questions to bring to the next Group Session:

Spiritual Warfare

LESSON #9

CLASSROOM DISCUSSION

Primary weapons of the enemy – how he wages battle against us

1. _____

2. _____

3. _____

How are the weapons of the devil used to attack a person (particularly a Christian) in the area of sin and how do we fight back?

Deception – "I have experienced negative things in my life and therefore, I am not loved."

_____ (Jeremiah 31:3)

_____ (John 3:16, Isaiah 43:18-19)

Temptation – to believe that whatever the enemy is dangling before me as an unholy temptation is what I need and want.

How do you combat the temptation to fall for the trap of the enemy?

_____ (James 4:7)

Accusation – if you submit to the temptation and go where you have no business going, the devil then accuses you and condemns you for your sin.

Which piece of the Armor of God should you use to combat the accusations of the enemy for your sin?

_____ of Faith.

What should you do when you fall into sin?

_____ and ask for forgiveness. (1 John 1:9, John 3:17)

Do not be afraid of the attacks of the enemy.

You have the _____ to cast out demons. (Luke 10:19)

NOTES

The Heart

LESSON #10

HOMEWORK

When Scripture refers to the 'heart', it is usually not referring to the physical muscle in your chest that pumps blood throughout your body. According to the *New Unger's Bible Dictionary*, the word 'heart' in Scripture means a variety of things, including:

- The center of the bodily life, the reservoir of the entire life-power (Psalm 40:8, 10, 12)
- The center of the rational-spiritual nature of man (Esther 7:5, 1 Corinthians 7:37)
- The seat of love and hatred (1 Timothy 1:5, Leviticus 19:17)
- The center of the moral life from highest love of God to hardening of the heart (Psalm 73:26, Isaiah 6:10, Jeremiah 16:12)
- The laboratory and origin of all that is good and evil in thoughts, words, and deeds (Matthew 12:34, Mark 7:21)
- The rendezvous of evil lusts and passions (Romans 1:24)
- The seat of conscience (Hebrews 10:22, 1 John 3:19-21)

Many of the references above seem to be tied to <u>emotions</u>. Other references to the heart in Scripture reveal that it is also tied to the <u>mind</u> or intellect of a man, and it can understand (John 12:40, Ephesians 1:8). The heart is also tied to the <u>will</u> of man (Exodus 25:2, 35:5).

Additionally, the heart is closely connected with the 'soul' having, as one meaning, the seat of the feelings, desires, affections, and aversions of a man *(New Unger's Bible Dictionary)*. In other words, the heart is tied to the <u>conscience</u> of a man.

As you can see, the scriptural heart is very closely tied to the mind, will, emotions, and conscience of a person. God has said repeatedly in His Word that we are to love Him and serve Him with our whole heart (Deuteronomy 6:5, 11:13, 13:3, Joshua 22:5, Jeremiah 29:13, Matthew 22:37, Mark 12:30, Luke 10:27). In order to love and serve Him well, we must have our hearts right with God.

Proverbs 27:19 says, *"As in water face reflects face, so a man's heart reveals the man,"* Therefore, it is extremely important that our hearts are pure and clean. *Create in me a clean heart, O God, and renew a steadfast spirit within me.* (Psalm 51:10) We also must be very careful not to allow our hearts to become hard and incapable of receiving the love and affection of God (Ephesians 4:18, Proverbs 28:14).

If you have allowed your heart to become hard and calloused as a result of the things you have experienced in your life, there is great news! God is in the business of heart transplants and He says, *"I will give you a new heart and put a new spirit within you; I will take the heart of stone out of your flesh and give you a heart of flesh."* (Ezekiel 36:26)

This Week's Memory Verse:

Proverbs 4:23 (NKJV) *Keep your heart with all diligence, for out of it spring the issues of life.*

DAY 1

Read Hebrews 3:7-4:16 and answer the following questions:

1. Hebrews 3:7-11 (is a quote from Psalm 95:7-11) and is a warning for the Hebrew Christians about hardening their hearts to God and the salvation He offers them. The author of Hebrews uses the example of the Israelites who wandered with Moses in the wilderness for 40 years because they refused to trust God to provide for all of their needs. (See Exodus 17:1-7.)

   What is Hebrews 3:7-11 revealing to you with respect to trusting God to meet all of your relational and emotional needs?

   _____
   _____
   _____
   _____
   _____
   _____
   _____

2. Verse 7 says "Today, if you will hear His voice..." What has God been speaking to you about specifically throughout this study so far that He wants you to apply to your life to be free from the current bondages of sin?

   _____
   _____
   _____
   _____
   _____
   _____

3. Verse 11 speaks of rest. What does 'rest' mean to you with respect to bondage to sin? What would 'rest' look like and feel like to you if you entered into the 'rest' of God?

_____

4. In the space below, write a prayer to God asking Him to help you to clearly hear His voice and to soften your heart so you can completely trust Him to provide for all of your relational and emotional needs in a healthy, godly way so you can enter into His rest.

_____

Practice writing your memory verse (Proverbs 4:23).

DAY 2

Read Hebrews 3:7-4:16 and answer the following questions:

1. What does Hebrews 3:12-15 say about departing from the living God? What does this have to do with trusting God to heal you from your bondage to sin?

2. Why do you think sin hardens your heart (see verse 13)?

3. Have you personally experienced a hardening of your heart towards God? Explain.

4. What does verse 13 say about exhorting (encouraging) other believers? How does this help you (and others) to avoid hardening your heart towards God?

Practice writing your memory verse (Proverbs 4:23).

DAY 3

Read Hebrews 3:7-4:16 and answer the following questions:

1. What does Hebrews 3:16 – 4:7 say about healing from bondage to sin? Can you see the parallels between the Israelites being brought out of the bondage of slavery in Egypt and you being brought out of the bondage of your sin? Explain.

2. How do you think God feels when you don't trust Him completely to provide for your relational and emotional needs? (See Numbers 11:1-6.) How does this affect your heart (mind, will, emotions)?

3. Write a prayer to God asking Him to increase your faith and trust in Him to help you rest in the knowledge that He will meet your every need relationally, emotionally, physically, and spiritually so you will not be tempted 'to go back to Egypt' – even in your mind. Tell Him about your struggles and ask Him to heal you from the inside out.

_____

_____

_____

_____

_____

_____

_____

_____

Practice writing your memory verse (Proverbs 4:23).

DAY 4

Read Hebrews 3:7-4:16 and answer the following questions:

1. What does Hebrews 4:8-13 say about the rest that God offers to us? Notice in verse 11, the word 'diligent'. What does it mean to be *diligent* to enter that rest and how does this affect your heart (mind, will, emotions)?

   _____

   _____

   _____

   _____

   _____

   _____

   _____

2. Hebrews 4:8 reveals that the Israelites did not enter God's rest merely by entering into the Promised Land led by Joshua. How does this relate to overcoming sin in your life? Think about how the Israelites had to 'fight' for their new territory and continually trust God once they crossed over into the Promised Land. What do you have to continue to do to enter into the rest of God?

   _____

   _____

   _____

   _____

   _____

   _____

   _____

   _____

3. What does Hebrews 4:12-13 say about the Word of God?

_____

_____

_____

_____

_____

_____

_____

_____

4. Hebrews 4:12 says that the Word of God is a discerner of the thoughts and intents of the heart. What does this mean to you? Have you been convicted by the Word of God in areas of your life related to your sin?

    What would you say to God if you were standing before Jesus right now and He asks you if you will trust Him to completely deliver you from sin and heal your heart from the pain and scars you have as a result of sin in your life?

_____

_____

_____

_____

_____

_____

_____

_____

Practice writing your memory verse (Proverbs 4:23).

DAY 5

Read Hebrews 3:7-4:16 and answer the following questions:

1. What does Hebrews 4:14-16 say about Jesus?

_____
_____
_____
_____
_____
_____

2. What does Hebrews 4:15 say about Jesus' understanding of how hard it is for us to live holy lives in the face of temptations?

_____
_____
_____
_____
_____
_____

3. What is the good news in Hebrews 4:16? How does this relate to our heart (mind, will, emotions) when we are determined to set our heart right with God and not to allow the sins of our past to dictate how we live our lives today and in the future?

_____
_____
_____
_____
_____

4. In the space below, write a prayer to God asking Him to pour out his grace and mercy upon you as you determine to honor Him with your whole heart (mind, will, and emotions). Ask Him to keep your heart soft and tender so you can receive all of the love of Christ that He has to give you, which brings healing and wholeness to the areas of brokenness in your life.

___

___

___

___

___

___

___

___

5. Take a fresh look at your Timeline/Root Cause Exercise (Lesson #6). Is there anything else God has revealed to you this week that you need to add to it?

   Practice writing your memory verse (Proverbs 4:23).

   Notes/Questions to bring to the next Group Session:

The Heart

LESSON #10

CLASSROOM DISCUSSION

Emotional Relationships that Result in Idolatry

Some people never actually cross the line and enter into any kind of sexual relationship with another person who is not their spouse, but they are strongly tied to another man or woman in an unhealthy emotional relationship. These relationships go beyond mere friendship, and result in idolatry.

1. We are _____ when we trust in _____ to give us strength and allow our _____ to _____ from God. (Jeremiah 17:5)

2. We are to _____ from _____. (1 Corinthians 10:14)

   1 Corinthians 10:14 - *Therefore, my beloved, flee from idolatry.*

Hardening of the Heart

Some people, as a result of past hurts in their lives, have allowed their hearts to turn to stone as a defense mechanism to protect them from further hurt.

3. God will take the heart of _____ out of your flesh and give you a new heart of _____. (Ezekiel 36:26)

   Discuss Ephesians 3:16-19.

NOTES

Our Authority in Christ to Rout Demons

LESSON #11

HOMEWORK

If you have surrendered your life to Jesus and truly accepted Him as Lord and Savior, you already have the power and authority of Jesus' name to cast out demons and walk in complete victory over the attacks of the enemy.

We read in the Scriptures where Jesus sent His disciples out in pairs and instructed them to heal the sick, cleanse lepers, raise the dead, and cast out demons (Matthew 10:1-4; Mark 6:7; Luke 9:1-3). Jesus taught His disciples saying, "Most assuredly, I say to you, he who believes in Me, the works that I do he will do also; and greater works than these he will do, because I go to My Father. And whatever you ask in My name, that I will do, that the Father may be glorified in the Son. If you ask anything in My name, I will do it." (John 14:12-14). He also teaches us to resist the enemy and draw near to God (James 4:7-8). God is the one who will fight for us.

We are not to fear the enemy. Jesus has already defeated Satan when He was crucified, died, was buried, and rose from the dead, and is now seated at the right hand of the Father in heaven. Jesus will finally cast Satan into the lake of fire for all of eternity at the appointed time (Revelation 20:2-3, 7,10). Furthermore, God's Word assures us that nothing can harm us or separate us from his love.

> ^{35}*Who shall separate us from the love of Christ? Shall tribulation, or distress, or persecution, or famine, or nakedness, or peril, or sword?* ^{36}*As it is written:*
>
> *"For Your sake we are killed all day long; We are accounted as sheep for the slaughter."*
>
> ^{37}*Yet in all these things we are more than conquerors through Him who loved us.* ^{38}*For I am persuaded that neither death nor life, nor angels nor principalities nor powers, nor things present nor things to come,* ^{39}*nor height nor depth, nor any other created thing, shall be able to separate us from the love of God which is in Christ Jesus our Lord. (Romans 8:35-39)*

This Week's Memory Verse:

<u>James 4:7</u> (NKJV) *Therefore submit to God. Resist the devil and he will flee from you.*

DAY 1

Read Psalm 143 and answer the following questions

1. In the light of spiritual warfare, which verses are speaking to you the loudest? Explain.

2. Verses 3-4 says *"For the enemy has persecuted my soul; he has crushed my life to the ground; he has made me dwell in darkness, like those who have long been dead. Therefore my spirit is overwhelmed within me; My heart within me is distressed."* Is this now, or has this ever been the cry of your heart? What does the first verse of Luke 10:19 say to give you hope, and what do you have to do to apply that verse to your life?

3. Read Mark 16:16-17, John 14:12-13, and James 4:7. What do these Scriptures say regarding your authority to cast out the demons that try to hinder and divert you from walking in the plans and purposes of God for your life?

_____

_____

_____

_____

_____

_____

_____

4. In the space below, write a prayer to God asking Him to show you how to wield the power to cast out demons that harass you and to increase your faith to trust and obey Him - applying His Word when He reveals His truth to you in His Word.

_____

_____

_____

_____

_____

_____

_____

Practice writing your memory verse (James 4:7).

DAY 2

Read Psalm 143 and answer the following questions:

1. Verse 8 says, *"Cause me to hear Your lovingkindness in the morning, for in You do I trust; cause me to know the way in which I should walk, for I lift up my soul to You."*

    In Lesson #9 (Spiritual Warfare lesson) we learned about demonic bondages (lust, pornography, perversion, rejection, rebellion, hate, anger, resentment, etc.). When you experience this type of spiritual warfare in conjunction with your bondage to sin, what does David reveal that you should do in Psalm 143:8, especially regarding those 'spiritual doors' that may still be open in your life inviting the enemy in? What is significant about the morning? Explain.

    _____
    _____
    _____
    _____
    _____
    _____

2. Read James 1:6-8. When you ask God to help you close the 'spiritual doors' that have invited demonic activity into your life, what does this Scripture say that you need to do? Conduct an honest assessment. Are you completely trusting God? Do you truly believe that your prayer to close those doors has been answered?

    _____
    _____
    _____
    _____
    _____
    _____

3. Read Proverbs 3:5. When we believe <u>only</u> what we see with our eyes and feel in our hearts, we are not completely demonstrating faith in God. This is illustrated in the story of the disciple Thomas, who did not believe the other disciples when they said that they saw Jesus after His resurrection. Jesus appeared to Thomas later and said that we are blessed who do not see in the natural, but yet still believe (John 20:24−29).

Trusting in God and His Word does not always result in your 'feelings' changing, or you 'seeing' a change in your circumstances. But God wants you to trust Him despite what you see and feel in the natural because He is also working in the Spiritual realm to make lasting changes on your behalf.

In the space below, write a prayer to God regarding any 'spiritual doors' that are still propped open in your life (see Spiritual Warfare, Lesson 9, Day 5 Homework) and your complete trust in Him to close and seal those doors.

_____

_____

_____

_____

_____

_____

_____

_____

_____

Practice writing your memory verse (James 4:7)

DAY 3

Read Psalm 143 and answer the following questions:

1. Verse 9 says, *"Deliver me, O Lord, from my enemies; In You I take shelter."* Who are your enemies in the spiritual battles associated with sin?

   Aren't your enemies the lies of Satan who led you to believe that following your 'feelings' and people who satisfy your feelings is the way to a life of satisfaction and purpose? Let me be clear: the people you associate(d) with in your sin are not the enemy; they are just being used by Satan to draw you away from the truth of God's Word. It is the 'lie' that is perpetuated by Satan that is 'the enemy' that must be defeated in order to set you free from the bondage of sin.

   Do you understand the distinction? Explain.

   _____

   _____

   _____

   _____

   _____

   _____

   _____

2. What does it mean to 'take shelter' in God? Read Psalm 91:1-4. How do you visualize these verses? What can you think of in nature that demonstrates these passages of Scripture?

   _____

   _____

   _____

   _____

   _____

   _____

3. Write a prayer to God asking Him to deliver you from your enemies (the lies you have believed), to show you exactly what you need to do to bring lasting change in your life, and to shelter you close to Him as you grieve and heal from the wounds that have been inflicted upon you by the enemy of your soul.

_____
_____
_____
_____
_____
_____
_____
_____

Practice writing your memory verse (James 4:7).

DAY 4

Read Psalm 143 and answer the following questions:

1. Verse 10 says, *"Teach me to do Your will for You are my God; Your Spirit is good. Lead me in the land of uprightness."* David recognizes that he is unable to do the will of God without being taught how to do the will of God and by being led into uprightness.

    We, too, need God's teaching for our lives. Where do we obtain instruction about how God wants us to live our lives? Explain.

2. What specific things has God revealed to you that need to change about your life so that your life is aligned with His will for you?

3. What steps will you take to align your life with the will of God? Be very specific, writing down exactly what needs to change, what you will do, and when you will do it by.

   To help keep you accountable, be sure to share your plans with someone else who will pray with you and ask you about your progress. This is a great time to reach out to your Accountability Partner(s).

   _____
   _____
   _____
   _____
   _____
   _____

4. In the space below, write a prayer to God asking Him to help keep you accountable to follow through with your plans to make changes in your life to align your life with His will for you. Be brutally honest with God, telling Him how you feel about this.

   _____
   _____
   _____
   _____
   _____
   _____

   Practice writing your memory verse (James 4:7).

DAY 5

Read Psalm 143 and answer the following questions:

1. Verses 11-12 say, *"Revive me, O Lord, for Your name's sake! For Your righteousness' sake bring my soul out of trouble. In Your mercy cut off my enemies, and destroy all those who afflict my soul; For I am Your servant."*

   In this passage, David is pouring out his heart to God, asking for strength and telling God exactly how he feels. Is this the cry of your heart? Does it seem like the forces of evil that want you to remain in bondage to sin are overtaking you? If so, pour out your heart to God and tell him how you feel. After you do this, sit quietly and listen to hear what God has to say to you in response.

   _____

   _____

   _____

   _____

2. Read 1 John 4:4. What does this Scripture say about you and about God? Did you notice that the Word (NKJV) says that you *'have overcome'*? This is past tense, essentially saying that the battle has already been won! How does this apply to the spiritual battle that you are fighting to break free from the bondage of sin?

   _____

   _____

   _____

   _____

3. What is hindering you from completely breaking free from the demonic strongholds that have afflicted you as a result of your sinful behaviors (lust, pornography, perversion, rejection, rebellion, hate, anger, resentment, etc.)? Are you holding on to someone or something that you need to let go of? What are you afraid of?

   _____

   _____

   _____

   _____

4. God wants to free you completely from these strongholds in your life. He wants you to experience complete freedom. Read John 10:10. What does Jesus say in this passage about the enemy of your soul and about Himself? Do you believe that Jesus is able to free you and give you life more abundantly?

   In the space below, be honest with God. Tell Him about your doubts and fears and desires with respect to your bondage to sin. Trust Him to fulfill the promises of His Word in your life and vow to do your part to walk away from all people and things in your life that pull you back into sin and bondage.

   _____
   _____
   _____
   _____
   _____
   _____
   _____
   _____

5. Take a fresh look at your Timeline/Root Cause Exercise (Lesson #6). Is there anything else God has revealed to you this week that you need to add to it?

   Practice writing your memory verse (James 4:7)

   Notes/Questions to bring to the next Group Session:

Our Authority in Christ to Rout Demons

LESSON #11

CLASSROOM DISCUSSION

1. The _____ we fight and the _____ we use are not of this world, they are _____. (2 Corinthians 10:3-5)

2. To demolish the _____ that keep us in bondage to sin, we have to _____ God and change our _____. (2 Corinthians 10:3-5)

Daniel 3:1-30 – Notes:

3. We are to _____ _____ as a good soldier, _____ to Jesus Christ. (2 Timothy 2:3-4)

4. I am God's _____ and have already _____ the enemy because I have God in me and therefore I am _____ than the enemy who is in the world. (1 John 4:4)

NOTES

Forgiveness – Part II

LESSON #12

HOMEWORK

Do you harbor feelings of guilt and self-condemnation for things you have done or failed to do, things that you still struggle with that you know are not pleasing to God, feeling as though your sins are unforgiveable? I have great news for you! Forgiveness is a not a feeling, it is a biblical truth. God's forgiveness is a gift to man as part of our salvation for the blotting out of our transgressions so we can be restored to Him through the shed atoning blood of Jesus Christ. God's forgiveness has erased our sins (past, present, and future) as if they never occurred (Isaiah 43:25-26; Hebrews 10:17; Psalm 103:12, 130:3-4).

This does not mean that after salvation, we will never sin again. God knows our human frailties and therefore He has made provisions for us. When we do mess up and sin, we are to go to God, confess our sins, repent and ask for forgiveness, and He is faithful and just to forgive us and completely cleanse us from all unrighteousness (1 John 1:9). God does not replay the sins that He has forgiven and bring them up against us over and over again. So why are we so hard on ourselves? Why do we feel guilty and condemn ourselves when we sin? Why do we play the movie over and over again in our minds? Maybe it is because it is so hard for us to forgive others and we believe that our imperfect forgiveness of others is equivalent to God's forgiveness of our sins. Or perhaps, it is because we don't fully understand and fully embrace the forgiveness that God has bestowed upon us.

I am not saying that we have to forgive ourselves for our sins. Self-forgiveness is not mentioned in the Bible. Biblical forgiveness is from God to man, and from one man to another. What we need to understand and embrace in order to be free from the guilt and self-condemnation related to our sin is the amazing grace of God. *"Grace perfects forever the saved one in the sight of God because of the saved one's position "in Christ." Grace bestows Christ's merit and Christ's standing forever."* (The New Unger's Bible Dictionary, definition of Grace) By grace, we are saved through faith in Jesus Christ (Ephesians 2:8). We can't work for forgiveness or salvation; these are bestowed upon us by the grace of God. We just have to have faith and believe the Word of God, which says that God will forgive our sins when we repent and ask for His forgiveness, and He will blot out the memory of our sin as if it never occurred.

Like I said at the beginning, forgiveness is not a feeling. If you don't 'feel' forgiven for the sins you have committed despite asking God for His forgiveness, you must accept God's forgiveness by faith. Think about the incredibly high price that God paid for the forgiveness of your sins. He sacrificed His one and only son, Jesus Christ, who shed His blood for the remission of your sins (Matthew 26:28; Ephesians 1:7). God will not withhold his forgiveness from you if you truly repent and ask for His forgiveness (1 John 1:9).

This Week's Memory Verse:

<u>Isaiah 43:25-26</u> (NKJV) *"I, even I, am He who blots out your transgressions for My own sake; And I will not remember your sins. Put Me in remembrance; Let us contend together; State your case, that you may be acquitted."*

DAY 1

Read Psalm 51 and answer the following questions:

1. This psalm is David's prayer to God after Nathan the prophet confronted David about his sins related to Bathsheba and Uriah (see 2 Samuel 11-12:1-15). What part of this prayer is most moving for you? Explain.

___

2. Do you think that David believes that God will forgive him completely? Why/why not?

___

3. Even though David had also sinned against Bathsheba and Uriah, in verse 4 he says that he sinned against God and God alone. Why do you think he pleads with God saying he has sinned against Him alone?

___

4. Is there sin in your life that you have not confessed to God, or for which you still have feelings of guilt or self-condemnation? Using Psalm 51 as a template, write a prayer to God in the space below, using the words of David and personalizing the prayer for your own sin.

_____

_____

_____

_____

_____

_____

5. Verses 3-4 says *"For the enemy has persecuted my soul; he has crushed my life to the ground; he has made me dwell in darkness, like those who have long been dead. Therefore my spirit is overwhelmed within me; My heart within me is distressed."* Is this now, or has this ever been the cry of your heart? What does the first verse of our memory scripture (Luke 10:19) say to give you hope, and what do you have to do to apply that verse to your life?

_____

_____

_____

_____

_____

_____

Practice writing your memory verse (Isaiah 43:25-26).

DAY 2

Read Psalm 51 and answer the following questions:

1. What is David asking God for in verse 10?

   _____
   _____
   _____
   _____
   _____

2. David recognizes that his sin has damaged his heart (mind, will, emotions) and only God can renew, restore, and transform his heart. Think about your own life and how your sins have damaged your heart. In the space below, write down how your mind, will, and emotions have been damaged by your sins.

   _____
   _____
   _____
   _____
   _____

3. What is David promising to do in verses 12-15 as a result of God's forgiveness? Do you believe that this response is pleasing to God? Why/why not?

   _____
   _____
   _____
   _____
   _____

   Practice writing your memory verse (Isaiah 43:25-26).

DAY 3

Read Psalm 51 and answer the following questions:

1. What does David reveal in verses 16 and 17 about God's desire when we sin? What does this mean to you personally?

___

2. How has your spiritual life been affected by your feelings of guilt, shame, and condemnation regarding sin that you didn't think that God would forgive you for or sin that you didn't take to God?

___

3. Sin separates us from God, and only God can forgive us of our sins and restore our relationship with Him. It is, therefore, imperative that when we sin, we immediately go to God with a humble heart and ask for His forgiveness. We are not to wallow in guilt and shame, but expose our sins to God by confessing them and asking for His forgiveness just like David did when he set the example for us in Psalm 51.

   In the space below, write a prayer to God asking Him to teach you about His forgiveness and asking Him to help you to be transparent with Him about your sins. Be honest with God if you don't 'feel' like you are forgiven in any area of your life. Ask Him to increase your faith and to help you know that you are forgiven.

___

Practice writing your memory verse (Isaiah 43:25-26).

DAY 4

Read Psalm 32 and answer the following questions:

1. This is another Psalm of David that is believed to be in response to his sin with Bathsheba and Uriah. What verse(s) speaks to your heart? Why?

   _____
   _____
   _____
   _____
   _____
   _____

2. What is David saying in verses 3-4 about his attempt to hide or cover his sin? Have you ever felt this way when you attempted to hide your sin? Explain.

   _____
   _____
   _____
   _____
   _____
   _____

3. What happened in verse 5? Do you think David felt relief when he finally confessed his sins to God? What makes you think that?

   _____
   _____
   _____
   _____
   _____

4. In the space below, write a prayer to God based on verses 1-5. Think about your own sin and personalize David's prayer and make it your own.

_____

_____

_____

_____

_____

_____

Practice writing your memory verse (Isaiah 43:25-26).

DAY 5

Read Psalm 32 and answer the following questions:

1. In verses 6-7, David exposes his heart and reveals his trust in the Lord. What is he saying in these verses that encourage you about confessing your sins to God?

   _____
   _____
   _____
   _____
   _____
   _____
   _____

2. There is a shift in this Psalm in verses 8-9. God is speaking in these verses. What is He saying that He wants you to apply to your life? What characteristics do the horse and mule have that are undesirable with respect to God and forgiveness?

   _____
   _____
   _____
   _____
   _____
   _____

3. What are verses 10-11 revealing about the joy experienced by the forgiven sinner?

   _____
   _____
   _____
   _____
   _____

4. Have you experienced God's forgiveness in every area of sin in your life? If not and you are still feeling 'guilty' or 'condemned' for any area of sin, ask God to increase your faith so you can trust Him completely and accept His forgiveness for this sin.

5. Take a fresh look at your Timeline/Root Cause Exercise (Lesson #6). Is there anything else God has revealed to you this week that you need to add to it?

Practice writing your memory verse (Isaiah 43:25-26).

Notes/Questions to bring to the next Group Session:

Forgiveness – Part II

LESSON #12

CLASSROOM DISCUSSION

1. If Jesus makes you _____ from your sin, you are _____ indeed. (John 8:36)

2. We are _____ by the blood of Jesus and are granted _____ of our sins according to the riches of His _____. (Ephesians 1:7)

3. While Jesus stands ready to forgive us of our sins, there are some prerequisites to receiving God's forgiveness. What do you suppose they are?

    • _____ (Matthew 9:13)

    • _____ (1 John 1:9)

    • _____ (1 John 5:14-15, Matthew 21:22)

4. When Jesus forgives our sins, He chooses _____ to _____ our _____. (Hebrews 8:12)

5. God stands ready to _____ us, and He is _____ and _____ towards us. (Psalm 86:4-5)

6. Nothing can _____ us from the _____ of God. (Romans 8:38-39)

NOTES

Removing Hindrances to Effective Prayer

LESSON #13

HOMEWORK

Prayer is the expression of man's dependence upon God for all things. (The *New Unger's Bible Dictionary*). It is essentially our lifeline to God. It is vitally important then that our prayers are getting through to God, that He hears us and answers our prayers.

The Bible reveals a number of hindrances or barriers to effective prayer, which we will look at this week. If we can identify any of these barriers in our lives, with God's help we can remove them so we can effectively communicate with Him through prayer and receive the blessings and provision that He has for us.

God requires us to be obedient to His Word (1 Samuel 15:22). We can cry out to God day and night in prayer, but if we harbor certain sins in our lives, they will block our communication channel with God, and He will not answer our prayers. Some of the sins that create barriers or hindrances to prayer are: unforgiveness, unbelief, unrepentant sin, asking for things with wrong motives or contrary to the will of God, continued willful sin, pride, hypocrisy, and selfishness.

There are numerous examples where the people of God sinned and as a result, God did not answer their prayers or the prayers of those praying on their behalf. (See Joshua 7:1-12; 2 Samuel 12:13-23; 1 Samuel 14:37; Numbers 20:7-12, 27:14) Elsewhere in the Word of God, we are told explicitly the things that will hinder our prayer life with God.

A healthy vibrant intimate relationship with God requires a clear communication channel between us and God. Let's examine our lives to see where we need to make changes to improve our ability to communicate with and experience intimacy with God, so we can receive the blessings and provision that come to us as a result of prayer.

This Week's Memory Verse:

2 Chronicles 7:14-15 (NKJV) *14if My people who are called by My name will humble themselves, and pray and seek My face, and turn from their wicked ways, then I will hear from heaven, and will forgive their sin and heal their land. 15Now My eyes will be open and My ears attentive to prayer made in this place.*

DAY 1

Read Matthew 18:23-35 and Mark 11:25 and answer the following questions:

1. What sin is hindering the prayers to God in these passages?

2. Why do you think that God will not answer your prayers when you harbor this sin in your life? Why is it so important to Him?

3. Examine your heart. Is this a sin that you currently harbor in your heart? Be honest with yourself and with God and ask Him to reveal it to you if it is there in any form. In the space below write down what God reveals to you about this particular sin and how it may be hindering your prayer life with Him.

4. In the space below write a prayer to God repenting of your sin and asking him to forgive you for the sin identified as a hindrance to your prayer life, or if you don't currently harbor this sin, that He will protect your heart from this sin.

_____
_____
_____
_____
_____
_____
_____
_____

5. What practical steps will you take to ensure that the sin you identified above, as a hindrance to your prayers, will not enter into or creep back into your life and block effective communication and intimacy with God? Be specific.

_____
_____
_____
_____
_____
_____
_____
_____

Practice writing your memory verse (2 Chronicles 7:14-15).

DAY 2

Read James 1:5-7 and Hebrews 11:6 and answer the following questions:

1. What sin is hindering the prayers to God in these passages?

2. Why do you think that God will not answer your prayers when you harbor this sin in your life? Why is it so important to Him?

3. Examine your heart. Is this a sin that you currently harbor in your heart? Be honest with yourself and with God and ask Him to reveal it to you if it is there in any form. In the space below write down what God reveals to you about this particular sin and how it may be hindering your prayer life with Him.

4. In the space below write a prayer to God repenting of your sin and asking him to forgive you for the sin identified as a hindrance to your prayer life, or if you don't currently harbor this sin, that He will protect your heart from this sin.

_____

_____

_____

_____

_____

_____

_____

_____

5. What practical steps will you take to ensure that the sin you identified above, as a hindrance to your prayers, will not enter into or creep back into your life and block effective communication and intimacy with God? Be specific.

_____

_____

_____

_____

_____

_____

_____

_____

Practice writing your memory verse (2 Chronicles 7:14-15).

DAY 3

Read Isaiah 59:1-2 and Psalm 66:18 and answer the following questions:

1. What sin is hindering the prayers to God in these passages?

___

2. Why do you think that God will not answer your prayers when you harbor this sin in your life? Why is it so important to Him?

___

3. Examine your heart. Is this a sin that you currently harbor in your heart? Be honest with yourself and with God and ask Him to reveal it to you if it is there in any form. In the space below write down what God reveals to you about this particular sin and how it may be hindering your prayer life with Him.

___

4. In the space below write a prayer to God repenting of your sin and asking him to forgive you for the sin identified as a hindrance to your prayer life, or if you don't currently harbor this sin, that He will protect your heart from this sin.

_____
_____
_____
_____
_____
_____
_____
_____

5. What practical steps will you take to ensure that the sin you identified above, as a hindrance to your prayers, will not enter into or creep back into your life and block effective communication and intimacy with God? Be specific.

_____
_____
_____
_____
_____
_____
_____
_____

Practice writing your memory verse (2 Chronicles 7:14-15).

DAY 4

Read Proverbs 28:9 and Hebrews 10:26-27 and answer the following questions:

1. What sin is hindering the prayers to God in these passages?

2. Why do you think that God will not answer your prayers when you harbor this sin in your life? Why is it so important to Him?

3. Examine your heart. Is this a sin that you currently harbor in your heart? Be honest with yourself and with God and ask Him to reveal it to you if it is there in any form. In the space below write down what God reveals to you about this particular sin and how it may be hindering your prayer life with Him.

4. In the space below, write a prayer to God repenting of your sin and asking him to forgive you for the sin identified as a hindrance to your prayer life, or if you don't currently harbor this sin, that He will protect your heart from this sin.

___

5. What practical steps will you take to ensure that the sin you identified above, as a hindrance to your prayers, will not enter into or creep back into your life and block effective communication and intimacy with God? Be specific.

___

Practice writing your memory verse (2 Chronicles 7:14-15).

DAY 5

Read James 4:3 and answer the following questions:

1. What sin is hindering the prayers to God in this passage?

___

2. Why do you think that God will not answer your prayers when you harbor this sin in your life? Why is it so important to Him?

___

3. Examine your heart. Is this a sin that you currently harbor in your heart? Be honest with yourself and with God and ask Him to reveal it to you if it is there in any form. In the space below, write down what God reveals to you about this particular sin and how it may be hindering your prayer life with Him.

___

4. In the space below write a prayer to God repenting of your sin and asking him to forgive you for the sin identified as a hindrance to your prayer life, or if you don't currently harbor this sin, that He will protect your heart from this sin.

_____

_____

_____

_____

_____

_____

5. What practical steps will you take to ensure that the sin you identified above, as a hindrance to your prayers, will not enter into or creep back into your life and block effective communication and intimacy with God? Be specific.

_____

_____

_____

_____

_____

_____

6. Take a fresh look at your Timeline/Root Cause Exercise (Lesson #6). Is there anything else God has revealed to you this week that you need to add to it?

Practice writing your memory verse (2 Chronicles 7:14-15).

Notes/Questions to bring to the next Group Session:

Prayer Blockers
Possible Reasons Why Our Prayers Are Not Answered by God

LESSON #13

IN-CLASS SMALL GROUP EXERCISE

We can learn a lot from the example left for us by others who are written about in the Bible. Look up the Scriptures identified below and make a list of the various reasons why God did not answer the prayers of people who prayed to him.

Scripture Reference	Hindrance(s) to Effective Prayer
Deuteronomy 1:45 1 Samuel 14:37 1 Samuel 28:6	
Proverbs 1:24-28	
Proverbs 28:9	
Isaiah 1:15 Isaiah 59:3	
Isaiah 59:2 Micah 3:4 John 9:31 Psalm 66:18	
Zechariah 7:11-13	
James 1:6,7	

James 4:3	
2 Corinthians 12:8 Exodus 33:20 Ezekiel 20:3	
Hosea 5:1-7 Luke 18:11, 12, 14	
Isaiah 1:2-20	
Proverbs 21:13	
Jeremiah 14:10,12	
Proverbs 1:24, 25, 28	
Jeremiah 11:11-14 Ezekiel 8:15-18	
Job 27:8,9	
Job 35:12,13	

NOTES

Holy Spirit's Power for Inner Healing and Sanctification

LESSON #14

HOMEWORK

Who or what is the Holy Spirit? I believe that this member of the Godhead is the least known and understood. We seem to have a much better understanding about God the Father and God the Son (Jesus) than we do about God the Holy Spirit. Let's learn about this powerful helper/counselor that has been freely given to every believer who has accepted Jesus Christ as Lord and Savior to guide our daily lives and transform us from the inside out.

There are several instances in the Bible when all three persons of the Trinity are mentioned together (Matthew 3:16-17; Matthew 28:19; 2 Corinthians 13:14; Titus 3:4-6). The most notable instance is when Jesus was baptized in the Jordan River by John the Baptist *"When He had been baptized, Jesus* [God the Son] *came up immediately from the water; and behold, the heavens were opened to Him, and He saw the Spirit of God* [God the Holy Spirit] *descending like a dove and alighting upon Him. And suddenly a voice came from heaven* [God the Father], *saying, "This is My beloved Son, in whom I am well pleased."* (Matthew 3:16-17)

The Holy Spirit (or Holy Ghost) is a person, not an amorphous 'it'. He is God. In Acts 5:3-4 Peter said *"Ananias, why has Satan filled your heart to lie to the Holy Spirit ... you have not lied to men but to God."*

The Holy Spirit has a very critical role to play in drawing unsaved people towards God for salvation. First, He protects us from being destroyed by Satan until we make a decision to accept Jesus Christ (Isaiah 59:19). Secondly, He convicts us by exposing our sin to us, so we know that we need a Savior (John 16:7-8). Finally, He regenerates us by bringing our spirit to life and giving us a new nature the moment we accept Jesus Christ as Lord and Savior (John 3:3-7, 2 Corinthians 5:17).

After we are saved, and the Holy Spirit resides in us, He begins the lifelong work of helping us to live the way God wants us to live. Our bodies become the temple of the Holy Spirit (1 Corinthians 6:19) and He strengthens us for Christian living (Ephesians 3:16). He fills us with His presence if we allow Him the freedom to fill us (Ephesians 5:18). He teaches believers all about spiritual things as we inquire of Him for assistance in understanding God's Word and His ways (John 14:26; 1 John 2:24-27). He gives spiritual gifts to God's children to be used to serve the body of Christ (1 Corinthians 12:1-11; Ephesians 4:12). He also produces fruit in us that demonstrates our love of God and our transformation from carnal to spiritual (Galatians 5:22-23).

In addition to all of the things listed above, the Holy Spirit also performs a life-long process of sanctification where we are healed and changed from the inside out (Romans 15:16; 2 Thessalonians 2:13). Sanctification requires a separation from the secular and sinful and setting apart for a sacred purpose (The *New Unger's Bible Dictionary*).

One important thing to know is that the Holy Spirit is a gentleman. He will not force change on you. But if you yield your will to Him and ask Him to help you, the Holy Spirit will expose areas of sin in your life so you can take those to God and seek His forgiveness, and turn away from that sin and begin living in accordance with God's will for your life. The Holy Spirit lives inside you as a born-again believer, and He has a direct connection to God the Father and God the Son. Isn't that an awesome thought? The Word of God says that He intercedes for us. He is your ultimate prayer partner! (Romans 8:26-27)

The Holy Spirit will also reveal areas of deep-rooted pain in your life, which is a result of injuries that you have buried deep within your soul. In order for you to heal from these things, you have to allow Him to show you the root of problem – where it originated. Once the Spirit of God reveals this to you, take that painful incident to Jesus for healing. You may need to forgive someone for hurting you, or take other actions that the Holy Spirit will reveal to you. Sometimes, we bury things so deeply that we don't even recall being hurt because we have blocked it out of our memory. If you want to be healthy physically and spiritually, you can't hold onto the pain you have buried in your soul. It has to be exposed to the light of the truth of God and released to Him for you to obtain complete healing and deliverance.

The Holy Spirit is a powerful advocate and counselor who is standing by to work mightily in your life if you will allow Him to do what He excels at. And that is to - help you to turn away from sin in your life, and to heal from past sin and pain that you are holding on to so you can fully manifest the fruit of the Spirit in your life.

This Week's Memory Verse:

Romans 8:26-27 (NKJV) *[26]Likewise the Spirit also helps in our weaknesses. For we do not know what we should pray for as we ought, but the Spirit Himself makes intercession for us with groanings which cannot be uttered. [27]Now He who searches the hearts knows what the mind of the Spirit is, because He makes intercession for the saints according to the will of God.*

DAY 1

Read John 15:26 – 16:15 and answer the following questions:

1. Who is the "Helper" that Jesus is referring to in John 15:26?

2. What are the Holy Spirit's roles in assisting us according to Jesus in our Scripture passage for today?

3. Read John 14:15-17 in conjunction with John 16:13-14. What is the powerful message these passages are conveying to you for your own healing from the effects of sin in your life?

Workbook — Lesson #14

4. In the space below, write a prayer to God asking the Holy Spirit who resides inside of you to show you areas of sin in your life that you need to take to God for forgiveness so you can cooperate with Him for your sanctification. When He reveals something to you, immediately take it to God, repent, ask for forgiveness, and turn away from practicing that sin.

5. What practical things can you do to increase your sensitivity to and awareness of the working of the Holy Spirit in your life? Be specific.

6. Are you committed to doing what the Holy Spirit revealed to you to increase your awareness of His working in your life? _____ Yes _____ No

7. Why/why not? Be honest.

_____
_____
_____
_____
_____
_____
_____
_____
_____

Practice writing your memory verse (Romans 8:26-27).

DAY 2

Sometimes, the work of healing doesn't occur all at once. There are instances in the Bible when Jesus healed someone, but the healing wasn't instantaneous.

Read Mark 8:14-25 and answer the following questions:

1. Why do you think that the blind man wasn't completely healed the first time?

2. If you read the above passage 'in context' by reading what happened prior to this passage, you will discover that the disciples did not have a full understanding of who Jesus was. This healing in stages paralleled their partial understanding of Jesus. The Holy Spirit would bring complete understanding in time. Have you experienced instances of this 'progressive healing' in any area of your life? Describe below.

3. Read Deuteronomy 7:22-24. How does this passage relate to the healing you have experienced thus far and the healing you still need to experience to be completely free from the effects of sin in your life?

4. In the space below write a prayer to God asking the Holy Spirit to reveal those things that you need to surrender to Him so He can begin to break down internal strongholds and drive out wrong thoughts and motives that are hindering your deliverance and healing.

_____

_____

_____

_____

_____

_____

5. What did the Holy Spirit reveal to you when you prayed? What are you going to do about it? Be specific.

_____

_____

_____

_____

_____

_____

Practice writing your memory verse (Romans 8:26-27).

DAY 3

Meditate on Romans 8:26-27 and answer the following questions: *Note: Today, you will likely need more time to complete this lesson than you normally spend so plan your time accordingly.*

1. What area(s) of weakness do you need to surrender to the Holy Spirit?

   _____

   _____

   _____

   _____

   _____

   _____

2. Making intercession for you in this passage means that the Holy Spirit (God) will pray to Father (God) and Jesus (God) on your behalf. Are you willing to completely surrender and let the Holy Spirit make intercession for you in the areas of weakness that you identified and those you don't yet know about? _____ Yes _____ No

3. Why/why not? Are you fearful? Describe your feelings about this in a prayer to God in the space below.

   _____

   _____

   _____

   _____

   _____

   _____

4. Settle yourself. Relax and invite the Holy Spirit to thoroughly search your heart and reveal to you areas that need attention in accordance with the will of God.

   Imagine allowing Him to go wherever He wants to and shine a flashlight into the recesses and corners of your heart. Let Him have free reign to search everywhere: inside the containers that have been sealed shut, inside the files in your filing cabinet, under the piles of dusty rubbish, up in the corners where the cobwebs are, underneath the bandages that have been placed on wounds, absolutely everywhere.

As you allow the Holy Spirit to move throughout your heart searching for things that need attention, He will begin to reveal things to you. Use the space below to jot down what He is finding and showing you. Write down everything that comes to your mind – don't worry if it seems silly or unrelated to this exercise. You are learning to listen to the Holy Spirit, your Counselor and Guide. If you make any mistakes, He understands.

_____

_____

_____

_____

_____

5. In the space below, write a prayer to God asking him to heal/remove what the Holy Spirit revealed to you above.

_____

_____

_____

_____

_____

6. Were you surprised by what the Holy Spirit revealed to you? Describe how it felt to let Him search everywhere in your heart.

_____

_____

_____

_____

Practice writing your memory verse (Romans 8:26-27).

DAY 4

Read Romans 8:26-27 and answer the following questions:

1. Has the Holy Spirit revealed any additional things to you since you completed your homework assignment yesterday? If so, write them in the space below.

2. Read what you wrote yesterday and today that the Holy Spirit revealed to you about what is in your heart and write down any additional observations below.

3. Now that you have identified areas of your heart that need attention, pray and ask the Holy Spirit to reveal to you specific things that you need to do to do cooperate with Him for your healing. Write your prayer to Him below.

4. In the space below, write the specific actions/steps that the Holy Spirit revealed to you to facilitate your healing.

_____
_____
_____
_____
_____
_____

5. Write a prayer to God confirming your commitment to do your part to cooperate with your healing and asking Him to heal you in accordance with the plan the Holy Spirit revealed to you.

_____
_____
_____
_____
_____
_____

6. In the space below, write down what action steps you will take to cooperate with God for your healing and put dates on them. Then share with your Accountability Partner what God revealed to you so he/she can pray for you and hold you accountable to your plan.

What I will Do	By When

Practice writing your memory verse (Romans 8:26-27).

DAY 5

Read Romans 8:26-27 and answer the following questions:

1. What have you learned about the Holy Spirit this week that you may not have known or fully understood before?

_____

_____

_____

_____

_____

_____

2. Do you fully trust Him to help you heal from the effects of sin in your life? Explain below.

_____

_____

_____

_____

_____

_____

3. Have you already experienced healing in any area of your heart this week? Explain.

_____

_____

_____

_____

_____

_____

4. In the space below write a prayer thanking God for placing His Spirit inside you to bring your spirit to life and to guide and direct every aspect of your life in accordance with God's will. Thank Him for interceding on your behalf when you don't know what or how to pray. Praise Him for giving you all that you need to be healed, delivered, and whole!

___

5. Take a fresh look at your Timeline/Root Cause Exercise (Lesson #6). Is there anything else God has revealed to you this week that you need to add to it?

    Practice writing your memory verse (Romans 8:26-27).

    Notes/Questions to bring to the next Group Session:

NOTES

Listening and Inner Healing Prayer

LESSON #15

HOMEWORK

Prayer is how we communicate with God and one of the most powerful ways that He communicates with us. One form of prayer that has the ability to completely transform your life and deepen your intimacy with the Lord is Listening and Inner Healing Prayer. This week we will learn the principles of this type of prayer and put into practice what we learn through guided inner healing prayer sessions.

Jesus came into the world to set us free from sin and the effects of sin in our lives. We read in Luke 4:16-21 that Jesus went into the synagogue in Nazareth and read from the scroll of Isaiah chapter 61 verse 1 (our memory scripture for this week), and when He had finished reading the passage, He said, "The Scripture you've just heard has been fulfilled this very day." (Luke 4:21). What Jesus was saying, is that God sent Him to heal our broken hearts, to give liberty to those captive and in bondage to sin, and to open the prisons in our minds that are constructed by Satan to keep us in bondage.

God wants an intimate relationship with you and He wants to heal all areas of brokenness in your life. He wants you to learn to trust Him and to bring all of your cares and concerns to Him in prayer. In previous lessons, we learned about communicating with God in prayer, and we learned some of the things that hinder our ability to communicate with God. This week we will learn how to sit quietly before God and allow Him to speak to us. There is nothing more important for our spiritual growth than being able to discern the voice of God and to allow Him to speak into our lives.

Each day this week we will be practicing principles of Listening and Inner Healing Prayer. You should plan to set aside at least 30 minutes each day where you can get away from all distractions and be ready to write down what God says to you. I pray that God will speak healing words to you that will transform your life and ignite a passion in your soul to continue to make Listening prayer a regular practice in your life as you continue to grow spiritually in your relationship with Jesus

This Week's Memory Verse

Isaiah 61:1 (NKJV) *The Spirit of the Lord God is upon Me, Because the Lord has anointed Me To preach good tidings to the poor; He has sent Me to heal the brokenhearted, To proclaim liberty to the captives, And the opening of the prison to those who are bound;*

Day 1

Set aside a 30-minute block of time and remove all distractions. You may need to go somewhere to get away from your normal surroundings. Have a pen and paper (a prayer journal or this workbook) to write down what God says to you in response to the questions that follow. Prepare your heart and mind to be still before the Lord. After you read each question, write down anything that comes into your mind without trying to analyze it. You may see an image, hear a song, be reminded of a Scripture passage, or just have an impression that something is being said in your heart.

1. Jesus, what do you want to say to me? (add blank lines for them to write after each question for each day of homework in this chapter)

2. Jesus please search my heart and bring up anything that needs your healing touch

3. If you were able to hear from God, write a prayer of thanksgiving for what Jesus said to you. If you were not able to hear from the Lord in this prayer session, do not be discouraged. You can try again tomorrow. Write a prayer of thanksgiving for the quiet time you just had and write a prayer of commitment to come back tomorrow to sit quietly before the Lord.

___

4. Read what you wrote down in response to questions you asked God. Does what you wrote down line up with God's Word? He will never contradict His Word.

___

Day 2

Set aside at least 30-minutes and remove all distractions. Read what you wrote in response to question #2 from yesterday. If Jesus revealed anything in your life that needs His healing touch, that is where you will focus your Listening prayer session today. If you were not able to hear from God yesterday, try again today following the instructions given on Day 1.

1. Jesus what do you want to say to me today?

2. Are there any lies that I came to believe as a result of wounding in my past?

3. What is the truth? Help me to renounce any lies I have believed.

4. Write a prayer of thanksgiving for today's Listening prayer session with the Lord

_____
_____
_____
_____
_____
_____

5. Read what you wrote down in response to questions you asked God. Does what you wrote down line up with God's Word and is it consistent with His character? Remember that He will never contradict His Word.

_____
_____
_____
_____
_____
_____
_____
_____

Day 3

Set aside at least 30-minutes and remove all distractions. If you have been hearing from God each day, keep asking new questions. If you are not sure you have heard from God yet, don't try to force the communication. The best thing to do is to keep coming to Him and sitting quietly before Him. Don't over-analyze the situation. Sometimes we have an expectation about what it will be like, and when it doesn't happen that way, we get discouraged. God wants to communicate with you, and if you remain open and expecting to hear from Him, you will be blessed when He speaks in a way that you can understand. Don't give up!

1. Jesus what do you want to say to me today?

2. Are there any unholy vows that I have made as a result of wounds that I have experienced? For example, did I vow never to show emotion because I was discouraged from showing emotion in response to a painful event in my past?

3. Jesus help me to break and renounce all unholy vows that I made in response to wounding

4. Jesus what would you like me to know about how these unholy vows have affected my life?

___

___

___

___

___

5. Read what you wrote down in response to questions you asked God

___

___

___

___

6. Write a prayer of thanksgiving for today's Listening prayer session with the Lord

___

___

___

___

___

Day 4

Set aside at least 30-minutes and remove all distractions. If you have been hearing from God each day, keep asking new questions guided by what Jesus said to you the last time you prayed. If not, go back over the lesson on Hindrances to effective prayer and conduct a self-inventory to see if you can identify anything that may be blocking your ability to hear from God.

1. Jesus what do you want me to know today?

2. Are there any areas of unforgiveness in my life?

3. Will you help me to forgive anyone (including myself) that I have not yet released to you?

4. Are there any burdens I am carrying that I need to release to you?

5. Read what you wrote down in response to questions you asked God

6. Write a prayer of thanksgiving for today's Listening prayer session with the Lord

Day 5

Set aside at least 30-minutes and remove all distractions. Reflect over this past week and your experiences of devoting time to Listening prayer each day. If you have heard from God, I am certain it was a wonderful experience for you. If you have not been successful in hearing from God, it might be that you still don't recognize how He is speaking to you. When you come together with others who are doing this study with you, listen to the ways that God spoke to others in the group. This might help you to see that God was speaking to you but you didn't recognize His 'voice.' Our relationship with the Lord is built over time, just like relationships between people. The more time you spend together, the easier it is to recognize their voice. If you are persistent in your desire to hear from God, He will speak to you in a way you can understand and know that it is Him communicating with you.

I highly recommend a book titled *Listening and Inner-Healing Prayer: Meeting God in the Broken Places* by Rusty Rustenbach, (NavPress, 2011). This book will walk you through the process of learning to listen to God for healing in prayer. Portions of that book were used to develop the Listening Prayer chapter in this workbook.

1. Jesus what do you want to say to me today?

2. Write a prayer of thanksgiving for today's Listening prayer session and write a prayer of commitment to continue Listening prayer sessions in the future for the continued development of your intimacy with the Lord.

NOTES

The Power of Sharing Your Testimony

LESSON #16

HOMEWORK

There is great power in the telling and hearing of a personal testimony regarding what God is doing and has done in a person's life. Testimony is defined as a declaration by a witness under oath, as that given before a court or deliberative body; evidence in support of a fact or an assertion; or a public declaration regarding a religious experience (The American Heritage Dictionary of the English Language). The Bible is full of stories about what God did in the lives of His people thousands of years ago, but don't you agree that it is a bit hard to relate to some of these stories of people who lived in a far different time, place, and culture than our own?

What if you heard from someone today, who you know and who lives right where you live, about something incredible that God did in his or her life? What if someone you know was healed of an "incurable" disease? Wouldn't that have a stronger impact on you than reading about King Hezekiah being healed from the disease that was supposed to kill him around 700 years before Jesus was born? (Isaiah Chapter 38) What about the testimony of a woman in your town who was barren for years, prayed fervently and then was able to conceive and have a child? Wouldn't her story have a much more powerful impact on you than reading about Hannah in the Bible who lived approximately 1,000 years before Christ? (1 Samuel Chapter 1) What about hearing the personal testimony of a man or woman who lived for years as a gay man or lesbian, and who, through the power of God working in and through their lives, has walked away from that lifestyle, and is now living free from that bondage?

Sharing a personal testimony brings healing and encouragement not only to the person hearing the testimony, but also the person sharing it. For the person sharing, it "seals it" and makes it more real even to them. Sometimes, we can go through something incredible in an almost 'out of body' experience where it doesn't become real and tangible to us until we hear ourselves telling the story, or see a video, or hear someone else tell it. Sharing a testimony also reminds the teller of what God did in his/her life, when in the future, they may be discouraged about something. Just remembering what God has already done in your life can encourage you to hold on when the going gets rough. If He did it before, He can do it again!

Personal testimonies can reach some people for God like nothing else can. To see living tangible proof of the power of God working in a person's life today might just be the thing that leads someone to Christ. And, by the way... Satan hates it!

This Week's Memory Verse:

Revelation 12:11 (NKJV) *And they overcame him by the blood of the Lamb and by the word of their testimony, and they did not love their lives to the death.*

DAY 1

Read Joshua 24:1-28 and answer the following questions:

1. Why do you think that Joshua recounted to the people the entire history of the Israelites just before he died?

   _____

   _____

   _____

   _____

   _____

   _____

2. What is significant about your history, and what can be learned from recounting the history of your life?

   _____

   _____

   _____

   _____

   _____

3. Do you think other people can learn from you and be encouraged by hearing your story?
   _____ Yes _____ No

   Why/why not?

   _____

   _____

   _____

4. In the space below, write a prayer to God asking Him to reveal to you the importance of sharing your testimony, and what He will accomplish through your obedience.

_____

_____

_____

_____

_____

_____

_____

_____

Practice writing your memory verse (Revelation 12:11).

DAY 2

Read Joshua 24:1-28 and answer the following questions:

1. What is revealed in Joshua 24:2-3 about what God did for Abraham and how does this relate to your salvation story?

   _____

   _____

   _____

   _____

2. How do you think Abraham felt when God asked him to leave everything he knew and go to an unknown destination led by God?

   _____

   _____

   _____

   _____

3. How did you feel when you first accepted Jesus and began to walk in this new relationship with God?

   _____

   _____

   _____

   _____

4. How has your life changed since you accepted Jesus and began walking with God?

   _____

   _____

   _____

   _____

5. If you had the opportunity to share your salvation testimony with another person, and only had 1 minute to share, what would you say? How would you convey your story in such a way as to encourage a person who is being drawn by the Holy Spirit to accept Jesus as Lord and Savior of their life?

   Write your 1-minute testimony in the space below and plan to share it with the group when we reconvene.

   _____

   _____

   _____

   _____

   _____

   _____

   _____

   _____

   _____

   _____

   Practice writing your memory verse (Revelation 12:11).

DAY 3

Read Joshua 24:1-28 and answer the following questions:

1. What is being conveyed to the Israelites through Joshua 24:4-13 and how does the message relate to your life?

   _____
   _____
   _____
   _____

2. Why do you think that God allows His people to experience the types of things that the Israelites experienced in the passages we just looked at?

   _____
   _____
   _____
   _____
   _____

3. Why do you think God allowed you to experience the things that you have experienced in your life, both good and bad? What can be learned from your experiences?

   _____
   _____
   _____
   _____
   _____

4. Names in the Bible have great significance. In Joshua 24:11 we see a list of names of the 'peoples' that came against the Israelites. The names of the seven 'peoples' that were conquered by the Israelites are seven 'spirits' that had to be conquered by the Israelites so they could acquire what God promised them. What deeper meaning is revealed in this passage about what the Israelites faced when they crossed into the promised-land?

NAME	MEANING	ATTRIBUTES
Amorites	Mountain People	Obsession with earthly fame/glory
Perizzites	Belonging to a Village	Limited vision, laziness, low self-esteem
Canaanites	Lowlands People	Addictions, perversions, people pleasing
Hittites	Sons of Terror/Break Down	Phobias, terror, depression, deceit
Girgashites	Clay dwellers	Focus on earthliness and unbelief
Hivites	Villagers	Vision limited to earthly inheritance
Jebusites	Threshers/Humiliate	Legalism, suppression of spiritual authority

Taken from http://shamah-elim.info (Shamah-Elim Bible Studies)

5. Do you recognize any of these 'ites' over the course of your life that had to be conquered or still need to be? Be specific.

6. In the space below, write a prayer to God targeting the remaining 'ites' in your life and ask Him to help you conquer them as He did for the Israelites.

Practice writing your memory verse (Revelation 12:11).

DAY 4

Read Joshua 24:1-28 and answer the following questions:

1. What is Joshua saying to the people in Joshua 24:14-15?

___

2. Have you determined in your heart to serve God? _____ Yes _____ No

   Why/why not? Be specific.

___

3. Part of serving God is telling others about what God has done for you, so they can grasp the real wonder-working power of God through your story in addition to reading about people in the Bible who they have never met. What is it about your personal testimony that could impact another person if you were brave enough to tell it?

___

4. Who would most benefit from hearing your testimony? Think about age groups, gender, populations, people in the church, people outside the church, etc.

_____

_____

_____

_____

_____

_____

5. In the space below, write a prayer to God asking Him whom He would like to reach through you sharing your testimony. Following your prayer, write down what He tells you.

_____

_____

_____

_____

_____

_____

Practice writing your memory verse (Revelation 12:11).

DAY 5

Read Joshua 24:1-28 and answer the following questions:

1. In Joshua 24:22-27, Joshua and the people sealed their covenant to serve the Lord. They had reviewed the history of the Israelites: what God had done for them over the years from the time He called Abraham out of the world to follow Him, through all of the trials and tribulations they encountered along the way, to the promised land where He planted them. Why do you think at this point, they were willing to make a promise to serve the Lord?

_____

_____

_____

_____

_____

_____

2. Look back over your life (review your personal timeline that you have been working on from Lesson #6) and make notes below specifically identifying the work of God over the course of your life (even when you didn't know Him).

Event	God's Role

3. After reviewing what God has done for you over the course of your life, are you willing to say "I will serve the Lord!"? _____ Yes _____ No

   Why/why not?

   _____

   _____

   _____

   _____

   _____

   _____

4. How would sharing stories about your life encourage others to come to know and trust God?

   _____

   _____

   _____

   _____

   _____

   _____

5. Are you fearful about sharing your story with others? _____ Yes _____ No

   Why/why not?

   _____

   _____

   _____

   _____

   _____

   _____

6. Has someone else encouraged you to trust God through the sharing of his or her testimony? If the answer is yes, what impact did their sharing have on your life?

___

___

___

___

___

___

Practice writing your memory verse (Revelation 12:11).

Notes/Questions to bring to the next Group Session:

NOTES

Exposing the Pain and Glorifying God

LESSON #17

HOMEWORK

Part of our healing comes from exposing our hurts, pains, and embarrassments instead of burying them. Just like a wound that needs to be opened up and flushed out to purge an infection, wounds that we have experienced in our lives due to things we have done or things that have happened to us need to be opened up and dealt with for complete healing. If we keep these hurts and pains buried, they are buried alive and continue to affect us both physically and spiritually. An important part of our healing process is being able to talk about what we have experienced and how we have been affected by it.

The most effective way to begin healing from your wounds is to spend time in prayer with God, talking to Him about what happened. Like we experienced in our times of listening and healing prayer, God will help you to understand how much He loves you, that He was there when you were hurt, and He will help you to heal if you are willing to expose your pains to Him. Just like a child who falls and skins his knee, run to Abba Father and show Him your pain so He can comfort you and heal your wounds.

Another important way that we find healing from the things we have experienced in our lives is to share those experiences and their effect on us with other believers. Spiritual growth is accelerated by our relationships with other Christians. How many times have you been encouraged in your own walk with God when another believer shared with you something that they went through, and how God helped them through it? We learn about faith and experience spiritual growth by interacting with other believers.

There are many instances in the Bible where we see God enabling believers to encourage one another and be transparent with one another about their real struggles. A few of these passages follow: Hebrews 10:24-25; Matthew 18:20; Romans 7:15-25; and James 5:16. If you hold on to your hurts and are not transparent about your experiences and pains, you are masking the truth and may hinder another person's spiritual growth, in addition to delaying your own healing. It is easy for a person who has buried their own pain to believe that they are the only one who has faced what they have experienced. If nobody else is talking about what they have experienced, they may feel all alone in their pain. Once it is exposed to the light, healing begins.

Won't you commit this week to experience healing in some area of your life by exposing an unhealed pain, talking to God about it, and being transparent with another Christian believer about what you have gone through?

This Week's Memory Verse:

James 5:16 (NKJV) *Confess your trespasses to one another, and pray for one another, that you may be healed. The effective, fervent prayer of a righteous man avails much.*

DAY 1

Read Psalm 107:1-7 and answer the following questions:

1. Write this passage of Scripture in the space below and personalize it. Make this passage your personal prayer to God.

___

___

___

___

___

___

___

2. What stood out to you most in this passage as you personalized it and made it your prayer to God?

___

___

___

___

___

___

3. What painful/embarrassing/difficult part of your life comes to mind when you pray this portion of Scripture?

___

___

___

___

___

___

4. If your best friend were to share with you that he/she is experiencing a similar painful/embarrassing/difficult situation that you have been through and overcome, what would you say to encourage him/her?

_____

_____

_____

_____

_____

_____

_____

Look for opportunities this week to share with another person something that God did for you – something to encourage them in their own walk with the Lord, or to help draw them to Him if they don't know Him.

Pray and ask God to give you an opportunity this week to practice sharing your testimony one-on-one with another person. Write down anything He tells you about this assignment below:

_____

_____

_____

_____

_____

_____

_____

_____

Practice writing your memory verse (James 5:16).

DAY 2

Read Psalm 107:8-14 and answer the following questions:

1. Write this passage of Scripture in the space below and personalize it. Make this passage your personal prayer to God.

2. What stood out to you most in this passage as you personalized it and made it your prayer to God?

3. What painful/embarrassing/difficult part of your life comes to mind when you pray this portion of Scripture?

4. If your best friend were to share with you that he/she is experiencing a similar painful/embarrassing/difficult situation that you have been through and overcome, what would you say to encourage him/her?

_____

_____

_____

_____

_____

_____

5. Have you found an opportunity to share a portion of your testimony with someone yesterday or today?

_____ Yes _____ No

How did it make you feel (whether you were obedient to share or did not share when given the opportunity)?

_____

_____

_____

_____

_____

Practice writing your memory verse (James 5:16).

DAY 3

Read Psalm 107:15-20 and answer the following questions:

1. Write this passage of Scripture in the space below and personalize it. Make this passage your personal prayer to God.

___

2. What stood out to you most in this passage as you personalized it and made it your prayer to God?

___

3. What painful/embarrassing/difficult part of your life comes to mind when you pray this portion of Scripture?

___

4. If your best friend were to share with you that he/she is experiencing a similar painful/embarrassing/difficult situation that you have been through and overcome, what would you say to encourage him/her?

_____

_____

_____

_____

_____

_____

_____

5. Have you found an opportunity to share a portion of your testimony with someone yesterday or today?

_____ Yes _____ No

How did it make you feel (whether you were obedient to share or did not share when given the opportunity)?

_____

_____

_____

_____

_____

_____

_____

Practice writing your memory verse (James 5:16).

DAY 4

Read Psalm 107:21-30 and answer the following questions:

1. Write this passage of Scripture in the space below and personalize it. Make this passage your personal prayer to God.

_____

_____

_____

_____

_____

_____

_____

2. What stood out to you most in this passage as you personalized it and made it your prayer to God?

_____

_____

_____

_____

_____

_____

3. What painful/embarrassing/difficult part of your life comes to mind when you pray this portion of Scripture?

_____

_____

_____

_____

_____

_____

4. If your best friend were to share with you that he/she is experiencing a similar painful/embarrassing/difficult situation that you have been through and overcome, what would you say to encourage him/her?

_____

_____

_____

_____

_____

_____

5. Have you found an opportunity to share a portion of your testimony with someone yesterday or today?

_____ Yes _____ No

How did it make you feel (whether you were obedient to share or did not share when given the opportunity)?

_____

_____

_____

_____

_____

_____

Practice writing your memory verse (James 5:16).

DAY 5

Read Psalm 107:31-43 and answer the following questions:

1. Write this passage of Scripture in the space below and personalize it. Make this passage your personal prayer to God.

_____

_____

_____

_____

_____

_____

2. What stood out to you most in this passage as you personalized it and made it your prayer to God?

_____

_____

_____

_____

_____

_____

3. What painful/embarrassing/difficult part of your life comes to mind when you pray this portion of Scripture?

_____

_____

_____

_____

_____

_____

4. If your best friend were to share with you that he/she is experiencing a similar painful/embarrassing/difficult situation that you have been through and overcome, what would you say to encourage him/her?

_____

_____

_____

_____

_____

5. Have you found an opportunity to share a portion of your testimony with someone yesterday or today?

_____ Yes _____ No

How did it make you feel (whether you were obedient to share or did not share when given the opportunity)?

_____

_____

_____

_____

_____

Practice writing your memory verse (James 5:16).

Notes/Questions to bring to the next Group Session:

Exposing the Pain and Glorifying God

LESSON #17

IN-CLASS EXERCISE

Take 3-5 minutes and think about the first time you experienced a life-controlling sinful behavior

Write down what triggered it, what someone else did, what you did, how it made you feel, and what you now know about the root cause(s) of these feelings:

After knowing all you know now about what that experience opened up in your life, how would you warn a friend who reveals to you that he/she is experiencing a similar situation?

Pair up with a partner and share your testimony (5 minutes for each person to share).

NOTES

Tailoring Your Message for the Listener

LESSON #18

HOMEWORK

God uses people and their stories to draw others to Himself. Think about it: has anyone in your life ever shared his or her faith with you? If you are like most people, you heard the Gospel message more than once from several different people before you responded and accepted Jesus Christ for yourself.

In addition to drawing people to the saving knowledge of Jesus Christ through the sharing of the Gospel, God uses the stories of His impact on ordinary everyday people to give others hope, to increase their faith, and to bring them comfort. When we hear about what God miraculously did for someone else when we are in the midst of a struggle, or in the midst of pain and suffering, it may be just what we need to hold on a little longer and to actually believe it could happen for us, too!

God is working in the lives of his children – all of them – including you. He does not want you to keep to yourself what He has done in your life. He wants you to share it with others. He loves to hear His children talking about what an incredible God He is and what He has done for them. Think about how good it feels to hear someone talking to someone else about what a good friend you are, what a good parent you are, and what great things you have done for them.

When we share what God has done in our lives, we need to tailor the message to the listener. What I mean is the story of what God did for you doesn't change, but in order to communicate that well, you need to modify the story a bit to get the message across in the most powerful and effective way to various audiences.

Here is an example. When sharing your salvation testimony with someone who has never been in a church before, it would be ineffective to use "church" words like salvation, saved, blood of the Lamb, etc. because they won't know what you are talking about and may think you are a little crazy. It is much more effective to just tell the story using everyday words that they can understand, like "I used to live a self-centered life. I was never satisfied and always wondered why I was even here. I discovered that I was a sinner and that my sins were separating me from God. That is when I met Jesus. He died to take away my sins and to restore my relationship with God. I asked Jesus for forgiveness and He restored me to God and my whole life has changed! I now have a peace that I never knew before..." You get the idea?

We also need to be careful to tailor our testimony to listeners based on their age, their maturity level, etc. This is especially important when sharing your deliverance testimony. Only include the details that are appropriate for the listener. This week, we will study various instances where Paul shared his testimony to get some insight on how to do this.

This Week's Memory Verse:

1 Corinthians 9:22 (NKJV) *to the weak I became as weak, that I might win the weak. I have become all things to all men, that I might by all means save some.*

DAY 1

Read Acts 9:1-31 and answer the following questions:

1. Verses 1-19 tell the story of Saul's conversion from a man who hated Christians (followers of "The Way") so much he was plotting to imprison and kill them after obtaining permission from the Jewish High Priest – to Paul (God changed his name from Saul to Paul), a man who God would use to reach thousands of people for Christ in his time, and millions more over the generations that followed through his writing of much of the New Testament.

   What stands out most to you in verses 1-19? Do you see any parallels with your own life? Write your observations below.

   _____

   _____

   _____

   _____

   _____

   _____

2. Did you notice that at the same time God was working powerfully in Saul/Paul's life, he was also working in Ananias' life to bring these men together supernaturally to fulfill God's will in both of their lives? When and how have you experienced something like this in your own life?

   _____

   _____

   _____

   _____

   _____

   _____

3. In verse 15, God reveals to Ananias what He was about to do in Saul/Paul's life. Paul's commission (assignment) would include speaking to Gentiles (non-Jews), kings (government leaders), and the Children of Israel (Jews). Every child of God has an assignment that he/she is uniquely equipped to accomplish for God. He has been preparing you for this assignment your whole life.

What has God been revealing to you about how He wants to use your life and your Testimony (story) to bring Glory and Honor to Him?

_____

_____

_____

_____

4. What do you notice about how Saul (Paul) responded to his assignment in verses 20-22? Do you think God was pleased with his response?

_____

_____

_____

_____

5. What did Saul (Paul) have to overcome when he encountered the disciples in Jerusalem (verses 26-31), and who stood up for him?

_____

_____

_____

_____

6. Have you thought about how people you used to hang out with, and new people you will meet might respond to your testimony? In the space below, write out possible responses to your testimony and how you think you will react.

_____

_____

_____

_____

Practice writing your memory verse (1 Corinthians 9:22).

DAY 2

Read Acts 21:37 – Acts 22:22 and answer the following questions:

1. Just prior to this passage of Scripture (in Acts 21:26-35), Paul was falsely accused and arrested. What did he choose to do in this difficult situation? Think about the crowd listening to his testimony. Do you think his testimony was having a powerful impact on these people? Where do you think Paul got his strength of character – not to shy away from proclaiming the Gospel?

___

2. What do you notice about what Paul said to the crowd in Acts 22:3-5? How did he help them to see that he could understand their desire to beat and kill him?

___

3. Why do you think it is important to connect your testimony with some truth in the listener's life? Think about one person you know who is not a Christian and has not accepted Jesus as their Lord and Savior. What could you say about your life as part of your own salvation testimony that would help that person to connect with you and your amazing story of salvation?

_____

_____

_____

_____

_____

4. What does 1 Peter 3:15 say? Write that passage of Scripture below:

_____

_____

_____

_____

_____

5. Do you feel comfortable sharing your salvation testimony? If you are fearful or reluctant to share your testimony with some people (or with everybody), use the space below to write a prayer asking God to help you overcome this fear. Tell Him why you are fearful and ask Him to give you a boldness to share the Good News with everyone He places on your heart to share it with.

_____

_____

_____

_____

_____

Practice writing your memory verse (1 Corinthians 9:22).

DAY 3

Read Acts 26:1-29 and answer the following questions:

1. What do you notice about how Paul shared his testimony with King Festus Agrippa that was different from the passages we studied on Day 1 and Day 2 this week?

2. Do you think Paul was doing more than just sharing the story of his conversion with King Agrippa? If so, what was he doing? Identify the verse(s) in this passage that support your theory.

3. What do you think is the most important purpose of sharing your testimony? Why does Jesus want you to tell your story?

4. Beyond your salvation testimony, what other areas of your life does Jesus want you to become transparent about so He can draw other people to Himself? Pray and ask Him to reveal this to you. In the space below, write your prayer of response to God.

_____

_____

_____

_____

_____

_____

_____

_____

_____

_____

Practice writing your memory verse (1 Corinthians 9:22).

DAY 4

Read 1 Corinthians 15:1-11 and answer the following questions:

1. In this passage of Scripture, Paul is speaking to the Corinthian church, which was a seriously troubled church infected with sexual immorality, wrought with people suing each other, and crippled by the abuse of their spiritual gifts.

    Does Paul write to them in this passage as a person who is spiritually superior to them and is now qualified to rebuke them? Explain.

    _____
    _____
    _____
    _____

2. What role does humility play in the sharing of your testimony and speaking to others about spiritual things? To what did Paul attribute his worth?

    _____
    _____
    _____
    _____

3. Read Ephesians 3:8-9 and 1 Timothy 1:15-16.

    What is Paul reiterating in these passages?

    _____
    _____
    _____
    _____

4. It is very important when sharing your testimony to give credit where credit is due. Just like Paul, you must always acknowledge what God did in your life and that it was not your own willpower or your own strength that enabled you to overcome what you have overcome in your life. In the space below, write a prayer to God asking Him to reveal to you what He wants you to say about your life that will have a powerful impact on others.

_____

_____

_____

_____

_____

_____

_____

_____

Practice writing your memory verse (1 Corinthians 9:22).

DAY 5

Read Galatians 1:11-24 and answer the following questions:

1. Why do you think it was so important for Paul to tell the Galatian church where he got his information from regarding the Gospel?

2. Why does Paul continually tell people about his persecution of the early church? Don't you think that would be embarrassing and he might want to leave out that part of his story?

3. What part of your story would you rather leave out when telling about what God did in and through you? Why?

4. Do you think other people may have the same things in their lives that you once did? Do you think if one of them were to hear your story, it might give them hope?

_____

_____

_____

_____

5. In the space below, write a prayer to God asking him to strengthen you so that you can tell your story (all of it) so that others might be free.

_____

_____

_____

_____

Practice writing your memory verse (1 Corinthians 9:22).

Notes/Questions to bring to the next Group Session:

Tailoring Your Message for the Listener

LESSON #18

IN-CLASS EXERCISE

Identify one family member or friend who you know is not saved (has not accepted Jesus as their personal Lord and Savior):

_____

Suppose that person walks up to you and asks you why you believe in Jesus? What difference has it made in your life? What would you say to them? Jot down some notes below:

We will have an opportunity to share with someone else in the group who will serve as a surrogate (stand-in) for the person you identified above.

After sharing:

- How did it feel to share your testimony in this way?
- Do you feel you could do this if that person came up to you and asked you the question tomorrow?
- What can you do to strengthen your testimony?

NOTES

Spiritual Gifts and Calling

LESSON #19

HOMEWORK

There are a variety of Spiritual Gifts listed in the Bible. Some are considered supernatural manifestations of the Holy Spirits' work through a believer; others are motivational gifts; and still others are considered ministry gifts. Regardless of what you call them or how they are displayed in a believer's life, they are all given to us by God and are to be used in service to other people and to bring glory and honor to the One who gave them to us.

The church is sometimes described in terms of the people who make up the various parts of the body. (See 1 Corinthians Chapter 12.) Each person in the body of Christ has a role to play using the gifts that God has equipped him or her with. No gift is more important than any other. Just as every part of the physical body is important, and the body doesn't function well when a part is missing or is not operating to its full potential, the Body of Christ needs each and every member operating in the gift that has been given by God to be healthy and whole.

This week, you will take a Spiritual Gifts Survey to determine what gifts you have been equipped with so you can begin to learn about your gifts and how you can use them to serve others. You can find Spiritual Gifts Surveys on the Internet or in Christian Bookstores. If you are not already using your Spiritual Gifts in service to the Body of Christ, make a commitment this week to learn more about your gifts and to use them as God intended. You will be blessed when you are operating in the center of God's will – and that includes operating and functioning in the unique gifting that has been given to you in service to others.

This Week's Memory Verse:

<u>1 Peter 4:10</u> (NKJV) *As each one has received a gift, minister it to one another, as good stewards of the manifold grace of God.*

DAY 1

Complete a Spiritual Gifts Survey provided by your facilitator, or one that you find online or in a Christian bookstore. There is no right or wrong answer; this is not a pass or fail test. It is designed to help you discover your God-given gifts so you can learn how God has equipped you to serve people as you serve Him.

After you complete the survey, read over the results and be sure to print out your results to bring to the next class.

1. Were you surprised with the results of your Spiritual Gifts Analysis? Explain.

2. If you have completed a Spiritual Gifts Survey in the past, are your gifts the same or different? Explain why you think that might be.

Practice writing your memory verse (1 Peter 4:10).

DAY 2

Read 1 Corinthians 12:1-11 and answer the following questions:

1. This passage of Scripture lists nine 'manifestation' gifts (verses 8-11) that represent a supernatural manifestation of the work of the Holy Spirit through the life of a believer.

   List the manifestation gifts below:

   - _____
   - _____
   - _____
   - _____
   - _____
   - _____
   - _____
   - _____
   - _____

2. What does verse 7 say is the purpose of these gifts?

   _____
   _____

3. What is the source of these gifts? How do you know?

   _____
   _____
   _____
   _____
   _____

4. What can a believer do to obtain one of these gifts? Explain. (See verse 11.)

_____

_____

_____

_____

_____

_____

Practice writing your memory verse (1 Peter 4:10).

DAY 3

Read Romans 12:3-8 and answer the following questions:

1. The gifts in this passage of Scripture are considered Motivational Gifts. List the seven Motivational Gifts below:

   • _____

   • _____

   • _____

   • _____

   • _____

   • _____

   • _____

2. Why do you think these gifts are considered "motivational" gifts? Explain.

   _____

   _____

   _____

   _____

3. The motivational gifts are gifts that we possess. You may recognize yourself in one or more of these areas and know that you have been that way your whole life. List your primary motivational gift or gifts below and briefly describe how these gifts from God have been prevalent in your life even before you became a Christian.

   _____

   _____

   _____

   _____

   Practice writing your memory verse (1 Peter 4:10).

DAY 4

Read Ephesians 4:7-16 and answer the following questions:

1. The gifts in this passage of Scripture are the Ministry Gifts. List the five Ministry Gifts below.

    - _____
    - _____
    - _____
    - _____
    - _____

2. Who gives these gifts to people? What verse tells you this?

    _____
    _____

3. What is the purpose of the Ministry Gifts? What verses tell you this?

    _____
    _____
    _____
    _____
    _____

4. Is every believer equipped with one or more of these five Ministry Gifts? Explain.

    _____
    _____
    _____
    _____

    Practice writing your memory verse (1 Peter 4:10).

DAY 5

Read 1 Corinthians 12:28-30 and answer the following questions:

1. In this passage of Scripture, Paul uses examples of gifts from the three categories of gifts we have identified over the past three days. Try filling in the chart below with the nine gifts identified in 1 Corinthians 12:28−30.

Motivational Gifts	Ministry Gifts	Manifestation Gifts

2. What combination of gifts has God uniquely equipped you with?

3. Are you currently using your gifts in service to others? Why or why not?

4. What practical steps will you take to begin learning more about your spiritual gifts and how God wants you to use them to bring glory and honor to Him?

_____

_____

_____

_____

_____

5. In the space below, write a prayer to God asking him to teach you more about the gifts He has given to you and how He wants you to use your gifts for His service.

_____

_____

_____

_____

_____

Practice writing your memory verse (1 Peter 4:10).

Notes/Questions to bring to the next Group Session:

NOTES

Witnessing – The Great Commission

LESSON #20

HOMEWORK

After Jesus was raised from the dead and appeared to his disciples, He commissioned them to make disciples of all the nations. He told them to baptize believers in the name of the Father and of the Son and of the Holy Spirit, teaching believers to observe all of the things He had commanded them.

Jesus also calls us to make disciples by sharing the great news of the Gospel with unbelievers. Every believer is commanded by Jesus to share the Gospel with unbelievers (Matthew 28:19; Mark 16:15; Luke 24:47; and John 20:21). This is not just a job for Pastors and Ministers. You and I are to share the Gospel as well, and the Holy Spirit will enable you to share it with His power (Acts 1:8).

Do you remember who led you to Christ? Perhaps you heard a sermon or read a book that pricked your heart, or maybe someone shared the good news with you one-on-one. One way to lead a person to Christ is to follow a series of Scriptures known as the "Romans Road." The book of Romans lays out the Gospel message in an easy to understand story.

The Romans Road story begins by revealing the current state of the unsaved. We are all born into sin as a result of the sin of Adam and Eve in the Garden of Eden. The story goes on to reveal the demonstration of the amazing love of Jesus Christ for all men, that while we were still living in sin, Jesus Christ died on the cross to take away the sins of the world. The only requirement for a man to be saved is to accept the free gift of salvation offered by God. There is absolutely nothing man can do to earn a right to be called a child of God and to earn salvation and eternal life. This is a free gift offered by God to any person who recognizes the sacrificial death of Jesus, and who believes by faith alone that Jesus died for them. When that person calls on the name of the Lord Jesus Christ, he/she WILL be saved.

This is the great news of the Gospel. Every child of God is commanded to share this Good News with others. This week, we will study the Scriptures associated with the Romans Road and learn to share the Gospel as God commands us.

This Week's Memory Verse:

Matthew 28:19-20 (NKJV) *¹⁹Go therefore and make disciples of all the nations, baptizing them in the name of the Father and of the Son and of the Holy Spirit, ²⁰teaching them to observe all things that I have commanded you; and lo, I am with you always, even to the end of the age."* Amen.

DAY 1

Read Matthew Chapter 28 and answer the following questions:

1. What did Jesus command the disciples to do?

2. Did Jesus commission them to share the good news (Gospel) on their own? How do you know?

3. Do you believe this passage of Scripture applies to you today? Explain.

4. What did Jesus promise for those who obey Him by sharing the Gospel?

_____

_____

_____

_____

_____

_____

_____

_____

5. In the space below, write a prayer asking God to give you the courage and ability to share the Gospel with every person He sends your way for the purpose of drawing them to Him.

_____

_____

_____

_____

_____

_____

_____

Practice writing your memory verse (Matthew 28:19-20).

DAY 2

Read Romans 3:10; Romans 3:23; and Romans 5:12 complete the following:

1. Write out Romans 3:10 below.

_____

_____

2. In the space below, rewrite Romans 3:10 in your own words.

_____

_____

3. Write out Romans 3:23 below.

_____

_____

_____

4. In the space below, rewrite Romans 3:23 in your own words.

_____

_____

_____

5. Write out Romans 5:12 below.

_____

_____

_____

_____

_____

The "one man" through whom sin entered the world is Adam (see Genesis 2:16-17; Genesis Chapter 3; 1 Corinthians 15:22).

6. In the space below, rewrite Romans 5:12 in your own words.

_____

_____

_____

_____

_____

_____

7. In the space below, write in your own words the entire message of Romans 3:10, 3:23, and 5:12

_____

_____

_____

_____

_____

_____

_____

_____

Practice writing your memory verse (Matthew 28:19-20).

DAY 3

Read Romans 5:8 and Romans 6:23 and complete the following:

1. Write out Romans 5:8 below.

2. In the space below, rewrite Romans 5:8 in your own words.

3. Write out Romans 6:23 below.

4. In the space below, rewrite Romans 6:23 in your own words.

_____

_____

_____

_____

_____

_____

5. In the space below, write in your own words the entire message of Romans 5:8 and Romans 6:23.

_____

_____

_____

_____

_____

Practice writing your memory verse (Matthew 28:19-20).

DAY 4

Read Romans 10:9-10 and Romans 10:13 and complete the following:

1. Write out Romans 10:9-10 below.

2. In the space below, rewrite Romans 10:9-10 in your own words.

3. Write out Romans 10:13 below.

4. In the space below, rewrite Romans 10:13 in your own words.

_____

_____

_____

_____

_____

_____

5. In the space below, write in your own words the entire message of Romans 10:9-10 and Romans 10:13.

_____

_____

_____

_____

_____

_____

Practice writing your memory verse (Matthew 28:19-20).

DAY 5

Read Matthew 28:19-20 and answer the following questions:

1. What effect has the obedience of whoever shared the Gospel with you and led you to Christ, had on you and your life?

___

2. Without looking back over your notes for the lesson this week, try writing out what you would say (in your own words) to share the Gospel with someone using the Scriptures of Romans Road. Don't worry if you get things out of order or don't remember the exact Scripture references. Just give it a try to see where you are now in your knowledge.

___

3. Now look back over the Scriptures of Romans Road in order to see how well you did. (Romans 3:10; 3:23; 5:12; 5:8; 6:23; 10:9-10: and 10:13). Where did you get things out of order or forget something important?

___

4. What practical steps will you take to perfect your sharing of the Gospel so you can participate in the command of Jesus Christ to lead others to Him?

_____

_____

_____

_____

_____

5. In the space below, write a prayer to God asking Him to increase your knowledge of Him and your boldness to share the Gospel with your family, friends, and acquaintances. Ask Him to give you opportunities to share the Gospel.

_____

_____

_____

_____

Practice writing your memory verse (Matthew 28:19-20).

Notes/Questions to bring to the next Group Session:

NOTES

Your Life's Purpose

LESSON #21

HOMEWORK

God has a plan and a purpose for your life. In addition to your personal deliverance and healing from the wounds associated with your bondage to sin, God wants to use you and your testimony to bring other people to the saving knowledge of Him. He created you, loves you, and has been preparing you for your Mission your whole life (Ephesians 2:10).

Just like Paul and many others in the Bible, God will use the story of your life to bring glory and honor to Him as you are obedient to do what He reveals to you. When we look outside our own lives and see our circumstances from God's eye view, we can see that He has been preparing us all of our lives to come to know and serve Him. Isaiah 55:8-9 says, *"For My thoughts are not your thoughts, nor are your ways My ways, says the Lord. For as the heavens are higher than the earth, so are My ways higher than your ways, and My thoughts than your thoughts."* God sees the big picture and knows exactly how He wants you to serve Him.

This week, you will write your personal Mission and Vision Statements. You will also revisit your personal timeline (Lesson #6), and instead of focusing on the past, you will project your timeline into the future to show the steps necessary to achieve the Vision God will reveal to you. There is power in writing down what God reveals to you. Just like the power of the written Word in the Bible, writing down the truth that God reveals to you as you pray and ask Him to show you how He wants to use your life, is the first step to seeing those plans displayed in your life.

Writing and continuously reviewing your personal Mission and Vision statements also helps you to stay focused on the things that God has uniquely gifted and equipped you to contribute as part of the Body of Christ. There are numerous 'good things' that you can be doing, but if they distract from the Mission and Vision that God has revealed to you, you will be less effective, and may get burned out. After you have your clear Mission and Vision from God, evaluate every opportunity that comes your way and see if it will advance or detract from what He has assigned you to do. Only participate in activities that move you closer to your Mission and Vision.

Please know that we are not saved by the works that we do for God. "For by grace you have been saved through faith, and that not of yourselves; it is the gift of God, not of works, lest anyone should boast." (Ephesians 2:8-9) Our salvation comes from the finished work of Jesus Christ and our faith in Him alone. The works that we do are a natural response to the amazing gift of salvation given to us by Jesus Christ, and the Word tells us that our faith without works is dead (James 2:14-26).

It is important that you don't miss a single day of the homework this week. You will be producing a personal Mission and Vision statement that you will bring to class to share with the others at the conclusion of this lesson, along with the new things God has revealed for you to add to your timeline.

This Week's Memory Verse:

Ephesians 2:10 (NKJV) *For we are His workmanship, created in Christ Jesus for good works, which God prepared beforehand that we should walk in them.*

DAY 1

Read James 1:21-27 and answer the following questions:

1. What stood out to you most in this Scripture? What is God saying to you?

_____

_____

_____

_____

_____

_____

_____

2. Read the Scripture out loud – this time personalizing it. Are you a doer of the word, or have you been a hearer only? What areas of your life have you been a hearer only?

_____

_____

_____

_____

_____

3. Pray and ask God to reveal areas of your life where He wants you to apply His Word to your life. Record what He is telling you in the space below.

_____

_____

_____

_____

4. This week we will develop our personal Mission and Vision Statements. God has a plan and a purpose for the life of each one of His children.

What has He been revealing to you over the course of the past 32 weeks that He wants you to do as a result of how He has been revealing Himself to you and His purposes for your life?

Take some time to pray and ask God to begin to speak to you about your future. In the space below, jot down what He is showing you, as well as any associated Scripture references He brings to mind.

_____

_____

_____

_____

Practice writing your memory verse (Ephesians 2:10).

DAY 2

Read James 1:16-18 and answer the following questions:

1. What gifts has God given you for advancing His Kingdom? Think of your Spiritual Gifts as well as the other gifts He has bestowed on you (material, physical, time, talents, etc.). Write in the space below all of the gifts that you have been given by God that He wants you to use to bring glory and honor to Him.

2. Where does the Scripture say that the gifts come from?

3. When the Bible speaks of first fruits, it is always in relation to giving an offering or sacrifice to God. What is God revealing to you that He wants you to present to Him as your first fruits offering?

4. Pray and ask God to reveal to you the Vision He has for your life (what He desires to see manifest in your life as a result of what He has done for you). This is a forward-looking statement that is not attainable yet. It is the desired result of your obedience to use what God has gifted you for to advance His Kingdom here on earth.

I will share my Vision statement with you to give you an idea of what I am talking about:

Vision: To see people delivered and healed from the bondage of sin through an intimate personal relationship with Jesus Christ.

My Scripture Reference: *Therefore, if anyone is in Christ, he is a new creation; old things have passed away; behold, all things have become new.* (2 Corinthians 5:17)

In the space below, draft your Vision Statement along with Scripture reference(s) that support your Vision.

_____

_____

_____

_____

_____

Practice writing your memory verse (Ephesians 2:10).

DAY 3

Read 2 Timothy 2:14-26 and answer the following questions:

1. What verses stood out to you the most in this passage? What is God revealing to you through this Scripture?

2. What does verse 15 say about how God wants us to live our lives?

3. Verses 19-26 exhort us to live our lives in such a way as to bear witness to others about God. What are some of the things this passage says we should do and avoid doing to help others escape the snare of the enemy?

4. Pray and ask God to reveal to you the specific Mission He has for you to attain the Vision He has revealed to you. This, too, is a forward-looking statement. A Mission Statement essentially answers the question "How will I attain my Vision?"

I will share my Mission statement with you to give you an idea of what I am talking about:

Mission: To draw unrepentant sinners and lukewarm Christians into an intimate life-transforming relationship with Jesus Christ by sharing my testimony and proclaiming the Gospel.

My Scripture Reference: *31And the Lord said, "[Debora, Debora]! Indeed, Satan has asked for you, that he may sift you as wheat. 32But I have prayed for you, that your faith should not fail; and when you have returned to Me, strengthen your brethren."* (Luke 22:31-32)

In the space below, draft your Mission Statement along with Scripture reference(s) that support your Mission.

_____
_____
_____
_____
_____
_____
_____
_____
_____

Practice writing your memory verse (Ephesians 2:10).

DAY 4

Read 1 John 2:3-11 and answer the following questions:

1. What verse(s) stood out to you the most? What is God saying to you in this passage?

2. Since we who believe and are saved by Jesus Christ are in the light, He wants us to live our lives in such a way as to demonstrate the light and love of Christ towards others. How will this be manifest in the Vision and Mission that God has given to you?

3. God has a plan and a purpose for your life. Everything you have experienced in your life up to this point has been preparation for the Mission and Vision God has for you. Read Romans 8:28 and write down what God is saying to you in that Scripture passage.

4. Pull out your personal timeline (Lesson #6). Pray and ask God to show you how your past relates to your future. Review your timeline to see all that God has taken you through and how your past relates to the Mission and Vision He has revealed to you. Write down your observations below.

_____

_____

_____

_____

_____

_____

5. Review your Mission and Vision statements and the Scripture(s) associated with each. Begin to write the future on your timeline (Lesson #6) – practical steps you can take to begin fulfilling your Mission with an eye towards the Vision God revealed to you. Add about 5 lines of space to record answer before memory scripture

_____

_____

_____

_____

_____

Practice writing your memory verse (Ephesians 2:10).

DAY 5

Read 1 John 2:15-17 and answer the following questions:

1. What part of this passage stands out to you the most? What is God revealing to you through this Scripture?

_____

_____

_____

_____

_____

_____

_____

_____

2. Pray and ask God how He wants you to serve Him. How is God specifically revealing to you that He wants you to "do His will"?

_____

_____

_____

_____

_____

_____

3. Review and refine (if necessary) your Mission and Vision Statements. Write both statements on one page along with your Scripture references in such a way that you can frame it and keep it on your desk or wall, in a place you where you will see it frequently.

   Bring your Mission/Vision statement to class to share with the other participants.

4. Pray and review your personal timeline (Lesson #6). Add additional practical steps you will take to begin fulfilling your Mission with an eye towards the Vision God has revealed to you. Plan to bring your timeline to class and to share with the group what God has revealed about your future.

5. In the space below, write a prayer to God asking Him to help you fulfill the Mission and Vision He has revealed to you this week.

_____

_____

_____

_____

_____

_____

Practice writing your memory verse (Ephesians 2:10).

Notes/Questions to bring to the next Group Session:

NOTES

Testimony Development

LESSON #22

HOMEWORK

We explored the power of sharing your testimony in Lesson 17, and learned from the Apostle Paul how he tailored his message for the various audiences that he spoke to while sharing his testimony in Lesson 19. Once again, "Testimony" is defined as a declaration by a witness under oath, as that given before a court or deliberative body; evidence in support of a fact or an assertion; or a public declaration regarding a religious experience *(The American Heritage Dictionary of the English Language)*.

This week, we will focus on developing our own testimonies related to our healing from life-controlling sinful behaviors. Over the course of this study, you have been developing your personal timeline (Lesson #6), which is essentially a record of where you have been over the course of your life, and the influences on your life that contributed to your sinful behaviors, and God has been healing areas of your life as you have worked through the exercises and completed the homework assignments.

Every person will be at a different place on the journey towards healing. Some have already experienced complete deliverance from sinful behaviors, and have reached some level of healing from the effects of those life-controlling habits. Others are still struggling, but can identify definite milestones along their path to healing. *There is, therefore, now no condemnation to those who are in Christ Jesus, who do not walk according to the flesh, but according to the Spirit.* (Romans 8:1) Every person has a testimony to share! When we share what God has done for us, He draws people to Himself through our obedience.

Sharing our testimony benefits us as well. It makes what God has done for us so much more real. Thinking and talking about where I came from and how far God has brought me encourages me like nothing else can! Speaking it into the atmosphere seals the healing. It puts Satan on notice that he no longer rules my life. I am now a child of the Most High God and He alone is sanctifying me day by day.

You can use your personal timeline (Lesson #6), along with the Mission and Vision Statements you developed last week to focus the content of your testimony, or use whatever method God shows you to develop the Testimony that He wants you to share. We will share our testimonies when we convene as a group at the completion of this week's homework assignment.

See the Testimony Development and Sharing Guidelines on page 297 of this workbook.

This Week's Memory Verse:

2 Chronicles 16:9a (NKJV) *For the eyes of the Lord run to and fro throughout the whole earth, to show Himself strong on behalf of those whose heart is loyal to Him.*

DAY 1

Read all of Psalm 91 aloud and complete the following:

1. Meditate on verses 1-3. How do these verses relate to the development and sharing of your testimony?

___

2. Pray and ask God what part(s) of your testimony relating to healing from your Same-Sex Attraction He wants you to develop for this lesson. Remember, your testimony is nothing more than the story of what God has done for you. Write what He reveals to you below.

___

3. Look back over your homework lessons in this workbook and see how far God has brought you! In the space below, write down notes regarding things you have learned and experienced during the course of this study that God wants you to share as part of your testimony.

___

Practice writing your memory verse (2 Chronicles 16:9a).

DAY 2

Read all of Psalm 91 aloud and complete the following:

1. Meditate on verses 4-6. How do these verses relate to the development and sharing of your testimony?

   _____
   _____
   _____
   _____
   _____
   _____
   _____

2. It is natural to have some level of fear and uncertainty when deciding to obey the will of God by exposing your life and telling others how God has dealt with you. In the space below, write a prayer asking God to help you overcome this fear.

   _____
   _____
   _____
   _____
   _____
   _____

3. Do you sense that God will answer your prayer and help you as you requested? Why or why not?

   _____
   _____
   _____
   _____
   _____
   _____
   _____

4. What additional things has God revealed to you since you completed yesterday's homework that He wants you to share as part of your testimony? Write those things in the space below so you won't forget to include them.

___

___

___

___

___

___

Practice writing your memory verse (2 Chronicles 16:9a).

DAY 3

Read all of Psalm 91 aloud and complete the following:

1. Meditate on verses 7-9. How do these verses relate to the development and sharing of your testimony?

2. In the space below, begin to write out your testimony using the work you completed on Day 1 and Day 2 Homework. Develop your testimony related to your healing from life-controlling sinful behaviors. Plan on your testimony being about 3 minutes in length.

   Note: If you have not yet experienced complete deliverance and healing, please don't let that discourage you from completing this assignment. Develop your testimony around what He has done for you so far. Perhaps you were able to forgive someone you never thought possible; or maybe God spoke to you clearly and healed some area of deep pain in your heart during the Inner Healing Prayer lessons.

   Develop your testimony around what God has done for you during the course of this study. God works on each one of us in His perfect timing. He loves you so much and He never moves too fast for His children.

Practice writing your memory verse (2 Chronicles 16:9a).

DAY 4

Read all of Psalm 91 aloud and complete the following:

1. Meditate on verses 10-12. How do these verses relate to the development and sharing of your testimony?

_____

2. In the space below, write a prayer to God asking Him to help you to strengthen and refine your testimony. Ask Him to give you a boldness to share the broken parts of your life, and what He has done to deliver and heal you with others to give them hope and draw them to Him.

_____

3. What do you sense God is saying to you as a result of the prayer you wrote above? Write in the space below His answer to your prayer.

_____

4. In the space below, write your testimony again. Each time you write it, you will notice that God is leading you to refine it because He knows what He wants you to say to reach the particular person or people He will bring your way to hear it. Remember, your life is not your own. God bought you with the precious blood of Jesus Christ, and your life's purpose is to bring glory and honor to Him.

Practice writing your memory verse (2 Chronicles 16:9a).

DAY 5

Read all of Psalm 91 aloud and complete the following:

1. Meditate on verses 13-16. How do these verses relate to the development and sharing of your testimony?

_____

_____

_____

_____

_____

_____

2. Practice saying your testimony out loud.

   It should be about 3 minutes in length, so adjust what you plan to say accordingly. You will share your testimony in class when we meet next.

   Practice writing your memory verse (2 Chronicles 16:9a).

   Notes/Questions to bring to the next Group Session:

NOTES

Personal Plan to Continue Daily Devotional

LESSON #23

HOMEWORK

You have been on quite a journey! Look at how far you have come in your spiritual growth and in your healing from the effects of your life-controlling sinful behaviors, and the development of a deeper intimacy with Jesus. This is just the beginning of the rest of your life, and I know that God has a great plan and purpose for your life.

You have been disciplined in studying the Word of God, as you have completed the homework and in-class exercises over the course of this series. Now, it is time for you to develop your own plan to continue abiding in Jesus Christ and His Word for continual growth and healing. God's Word is powerful and it heals and changes lives. *"For the word of God is living and powerful, and sharper than any two-edged sword, piercing even to the division of soul and spirit, and of joints and marrow, and is a discerner of the thoughts and intents of the heart."* (Hebrews 4:12)

Continued spiritual growth requires discipline. God wants to maintain an intimate and personal relationship with you. He has so much more for your life, and in order for Him to continue to heal your wounds and produce fruit in your life, you have to continue to abide in Him. Jesus says, *"Abide in Me, and I in you. As the branch cannot bear fruit of itself, unless it abides in the vine, neither can you, unless you abide in Me."* (John 15:4) He also promises that if you abide in His Word and meditate on what it teaches, you will be rooted, productive to the Kingdom of God, and prosperous, *"He shall be like a tree planted by the rivers of water, that brings forth its fruit in its season, whose leaf also shall not wither; and whatever he does shall prosper."* (Psalm 1:3)

God will continue to transform your life as He sanctifies you day by day if you remain in His Word, stay connected to Jesus and to other believers. No matter how far you have come over the course of this study or how far you have yet to go in your healing from the effects of your bondage to sin, the Word of God promises change and newness in your life, *"Therefore, if anyone is in Christ, he is a new creation; old things have passed away; behold, all things have become new."* (2 Corinthians 5:17) Walk in the newness of your life in Christ!

May God bless you as you continue your intimate walk with Him. I pray *"that He would grant you, according to the riches of His glory, to be strengthened with might through His Spirit in the inner man, that Christ may dwell in your hearts through faith; that you, being rooted and grounded in love, may be able to comprehend with all the saints what is the width and length and depth and height - to know the love of Christ which passes knowledge; that you may be filled with all the fullness of God."* (Ephesians 3:16-19)

This Week's Memory Verse:

Psalm 119:105 (NKJV) *Your word is a lamp to my feet And a light to my path.*

DAY 1

Scripture God placed on my heart to meditate on today:

1. Write down what God revealed to you in the Scripture He placed on your heart.

   _____
   _____
   _____
   _____

2. Pray and ask God how He wants you to stay connected to Him in the upcoming days and weeks. Write what He reveals to you in the space below as you develop your personal plan to continue to abide in Him.

   _____
   _____
   _____
   _____

3. What are some practical steps you will take to make sure you stay connected to God every day and remain connected to your brothers/sisters in Christ who have been such an important part of your life over the past 36 weeks?

   _____
   _____
   _____
   _____

   Practice writing your memory verse (Psalm 119:105).

DAY 2

Scripture God placed on my heart to meditate on today:

1. Write down what God revealed to you in the Scripture He placed on your heart.

2. Pray and ask God how He wants you to stay connected to Him in the upcoming days and weeks. Write what He reveals to you in the space below as you develop your personal plan to continue to abide in Him.

3. Begin drafting a personal plan in the space below. List practical things you can do to continue to abide in God's Word and to learn more about him. Write down specific things and dates/frequency. For example, I might commit to take one Bible Study Class offered by my church each semester. Write down the name of the classes you want to take and the dates when they start and end.

4. How will you keep yourself accountable to do what you planned? Write down specific things you will do to make sure you keep your commitment to God. For example, you might share your plan with a trusted brother/sister in Christ and give them permission to ask you about it at any time.

_____

_____

_____

_____

_____

_____

Practice writing your memory verse (Psalm 119:105)

DAY 3

Scripture God placed on my heart to meditate on today:

1. Write down what God revealed to you in the Scripture He placed on your heart.

___

2. Pray and ask God how He wants you to stay connected to Him in the upcoming days and weeks. Write what He reveals to you in the space below as you develop your personal plan to continue to abide in Him.

___

3. Continue drafting your personal plan in the space below. List practical things you can do to continue to abide in God's Word and to learn more about him. Write down specific things and dates/frequency. For example, I might sign up for daily email devotionals. That way, the Word of God gets delivered to my email account each and every day.

_____
_____
_____
_____
_____
_____
_____
_____
_____
_____
_____
_____
_____

Practice writing your memory verse (Psalm 119:105).

DAY 4

Scripture God placed on my heart to meditate on today:

1. Write down what God revealed to you in the Scripture He placed on your heart.

2. Pray and ask God how He wants you to stay connected to Him in the upcoming days and weeks. Write what He reveals to you in the space below as you develop your personal plan to continue to abide in Him.

3. Continue drafting your personal plan in the space below. List practical things you can do to continue to abide in God's Word and stay connected to the Body of Christ. For example, I might commit to join a specific Ministry where I can exercise my Spiritual Gift(s). I would write down when that Ministry meets, when I will get connected, and what I will do to serve.

_____

_____

_____

_____

_____

_____

_____

_____

Practice writing your memory verse (Psalm 119:105).

DAY 5

Scripture God placed on my heart to meditate on today:

1. Write down what God revealed to you in the Scripture He placed on your heart.

_____

_____

_____

_____

_____

_____

_____

_____

2. Pray and ask God how He wants you to stay connected to Him in the upcoming days and weeks. Write what He reveals to you in the space below as you develop your personal plan to continue to abide in Him.

_____

_____

_____

_____

_____

_____

_____

_____

3. Continue drafting your personal plan in the space below. List practical things you can do to continue to abide in God's Word and stay connected to the Body of Christ. For example, I might ask someone to be my prayer partner. I would write down that person's name, and when I plan to connect with them/ frequency of prayer, etc.

_____

_____

_____

_____

_____

_____

_____

_____

_____

_____

_____

Practice writing your memory verse (Psalm 119:105).

NOTES

TESTIMONY DEVELOPMENT AND SHARING

Purpose

The purpose of our testimony development is to practice sharing our testimonies of deliverance and healing and of what God has done in our lives so far. Don't worry or feel discouraged if you have not reached a point in your journey where you feel like you are completely free from your bondage to sin! We are all at different stages of our healing. Focus on what God has done in your life to bring you to where you are right now. Something has occurred in your life that has brought you to the point to seek out this ministry – and kept you coming back…that is your testimony.

Guidelines for testimony development/delivery

Each person will have three (3) minutes to share their testimony, which should follow this general outline:

1. How was your life before - what happened?

2. How did God impact your life for change, deliverance, healing?

3. What is different about your life now?

It is best to write out your testimony, considering who your audience is (helps determine what parts of your story to tell and what parts to leave out). Don't worry about length on the first draft. After you finish, read it out loud, and time yourself from start to finish. You will then know how much needs to be cut out to bring it down to 3 minutes. The finished written transcript should be about 350 words for a 3-minute testimony.

After you have it down on paper – practice – practice – practice (with a timer – like the free one available at: http://www.online-stopwatch.com/) and refine it until you are satisfied.

FINAL THOUGHTS

Congratulations for staying on course and completing this Discipleship Program! I know it hasn't been easy, and there were many difficult assignments to complete along your journey. Sanctification is a life-long process and we continually need to surrender our lives to Jesus and allow His Spirit to guide and direct our lives.

If you have completed this course with other Christian brothers and/or sisters, you have other people you know to help keep you accountable and to help you to continue to grow spiritually. If you had one or more Accountability Partners to support you during the course of this study, stay in contact with them as you continue your spiritual growth without the structure of this weekly Bible study.

Connect with a Bible-teaching/Bible-believing church if you aren't already a part of such a church so you can continue to experience healing and wholeness through application of the Truth of God's Word to your life. Remember, if you are in Christ, you are a new creation; old things have passed away and all things have become new! (2 Corinthians 5:17) Walk in the newness of your life in Christ!

Answers to In-Class Discussions

Lesson #1 – Classroom Discussion Answers 300

Lesson #2 – Classroom Discussion Answers 301

Lesson #3 – Classroom Discussion Answers 302

Lesson #4 – Classroom Discussion Answers 303

Lesson #5 – Classroom Discussion Answers 304

Lesson #7 – Classroom Discussion Answers 305

Lesson #8 – Classroom Discussion Answers 306

Lesson #9 – Classroom Discussion Answers 307

Lesson #10 – Classroom Discussion Answers 308

Lesson #11 – Classroom Discussion Answers 309

Lesson #12 – Classroom Discussion Answers 310

THE WORD IS LIFE

Lesson #1 – Classroom Discussion Answers

Bible Facts

1. The <u>66 books</u> of the Bible (<u>39</u> Old Testament and <u>27</u> New Testament) were written:

   - By more than <u>40 men</u> inspired by <u>God</u>
   - Over a period of approximately <u>1600</u> years

The Power of the God's Word to transform lives

2. Scripture is profitable for <u>Doctrine</u>, <u>Reproof</u>, <u>Correction</u>, and <u>Instruction</u> in righteousness (2 Timothy 3:16-17).

3. The Word of God is <u>living</u> and <u>powerful</u> (Hebrews 4:12-13).

4. The Word of God is a <u>discerner of the thoughts</u> and <u>intents</u> of the heart (Hebrews 4:12-13).

5. The Word will <u>transform</u> your life if you <u>apply</u> what you learn to your life (James 1:21-25).

6. We are to be <u>doers</u> of the Word and not <u>hearers</u> only (James 1:21-25).

THE ENEMY'S LIES vs. GOD'S TRUTH

Lesson #2 – Classroom Discussion Answers

The Enemy Has Been Trying to Destroy You

1. Your <u>adversary</u>, the devil, walks about like a <u>roaring lion</u> seeking to devour (1 Peter 5:8).

2. Our <u>enemy</u> is the <u>accuser</u> of the brethren, who stands before <u>God</u> day and night pointing out what we have done wrong (Rev 12:10).

3. The <u>enemy</u> desires to <u>sift</u> us as <u>wheat</u>, but Jesus <u>prays</u> for us that our <u>faith</u> may not fail (Luke 22:31).

4. Before God <u>formed</u> you in your mother's womb, He <u>knew</u> you, and He <u>sanctified</u> you (Jeremiah 1:5, and Psalm 139:13).

5. <u>All</u> things work together for <u>good</u> to those who <u>love God</u> and are <u>the called</u> according to His <u>purpose</u>. For those He <u>foreknew</u> he also <u>predestined</u> to be conformed to the <u>image</u> of Jesus (Romans 8:28-29).

6. <u>God</u> knows the thoughts He thinks towards you, <u>thoughts</u> of <u>peace</u> and not <u>evil</u> – to give you a <u>future</u> and a <u>hope</u> (Jeremiah 29:11).

7. You are to be <u>strengthened</u> with might through <u>His Spirit</u> in the <u>inner</u> man, that <u>Christ</u> may dwell in your heart through <u>faith</u>, being <u>rooted</u> and <u>grounded</u> in love you may be able to comprehend what is the <u>width</u> and <u>length</u> and <u>depth</u> and <u>height</u> – to <u>know</u> the love of <u>Christ</u> (Eph 3:16-19).

FREEDOM IN TRUTH

Lesson #3 – Classroom Discussion Answers

1. Jesus does not <u>condemn</u> sinners – He <u>forgives</u> them (John 8:1-11).

2. When we encounter Jesus and our <u>sins</u> are exposed to Him. He <u>forgives</u> our <u>sins</u> and tells us to go and <u>sin no more</u> (John 8:11).

3. If we <u>confess</u> our <u>sins</u>, He is faithful and just to <u>forgive</u> us our <u>sins</u> and <u>cleanse</u> us from all <u>unrighteousness</u> (1 John 1:9).

4. Jesus reacts to our <u>repentance</u> with <u>forgiveness</u> and <u>mercy</u> (Luke 7:44-50).

5. <u>Faith</u> in Jesus is what saves us and gives us <u>peace</u> (Luke 7:50).

HEARING GOD'S VOICE

Lesson #4 – Classroom Discussion Answers

1. God <u>speaks</u> to us through <u>nature</u> (Romans 1:19-20).

2. God <u>speaks</u> to us through the <u>preached word</u> (Romans 10:14; 1 Corinthians 1:21; Acts 10:42).

3. God <u>speaks</u> to us through <u>signs</u> and <u>wonders</u> (Exodus 4:1-9; Acts 4:22; Acts 5:12; Hebrews 2:1-4).

4. God <u>speaks</u> to us when we <u>worship</u> Him (John 4:24; James 4:6; Acts 17:24-25).

5. God <u>speaks</u> to us through <u>circumstances</u> (Acts 16:16-34).

6. God <u>speaks</u> to us through his <u>Word</u> (2 Tim 3:16; James 1:21-25).

PRAYER – COMMUNICATING WITH GOD

Lesson #5 – Classroom Discussion Answers

Our Prayers Move God on our Behalf

1. God will <u>incline</u> His <u>ear</u> towards us when we pray (Psalm 116:2; Psalm 17:6; Psalm 10:17; 1 Peter 3:12).

2. God will sometimes answer our prayers before we <u>finish praying</u> (Isaiah 65:24).

3. God <u>hears</u> the prayers of the <u>afflicted</u> (Psalm 22:24; Jonah 2:2,7).

4. When we <u>humble</u> ourselves, and <u>pray</u>, and <u>turn</u> from our <u>wicked</u> ways, God will <u>hear</u> us (2 Chronicles 7:14).

Power of Praying Scripture Back to God

5. You can be <u>confident</u> that God will <u>do</u> what He has said in His <u>Word</u> (Isaiah 55:11).

6. When God has <u>promised</u> something specific in Scripture we can be <u>confident</u> that <u>God</u> will answer that prayer (Deuteronomy 30:2-5/Nehemiah 1:9).

Jesus Intercedes (Prays) on our Behalf

7. Jesus <u>prays</u> for <u>all</u> believers to be <u>unified</u> with Him (John 17:20-26).

8. Jesus <u>intercedes</u> on our behalf as our <u>High Priest</u> (Hebrews 7:25; 1 John 2:1).

9. <u>Jesus</u> is at the <u>right hand</u> of the Father <u>interceding</u> on our behalf (Romans 8:34).

FORGIVENESS

Lesson #7 – Classroom Discussion Answers

Lesson on Forgiveness – What Forgiveness is and What it is Not

(Adapted from Resolving Everyday Conflict, Ken Sande & Kevin Johnson, (Baker Books 2011) © Peacemaker Ministries).

1. **Forgiveness is NOT** <u>Forgetting</u> (Isaiah 43:25) - <u>Forgetting</u> is passive (letting a memory fade over time).

2. **Forgiveness is NOT** <u>Excusing</u> (Psalm 32:5) - Excusing says "That's OK", or "You couldn't help it, or implies in some way that what you did wasn't really wrong"

What Forgiveness IS

3. **Forgiveness is a <u>radical decision</u>** (Romans 5:8) not to hold an offense against the offender. It means to release a person from punishment or penalty.

4. **Forgiveness is <u>undeserved</u> and <u>cannot</u> be <u>earned</u>** (Romans 5:8) - and it is very often an Expensive Decision.

5. **Forgiveness is an <u>Expensive Decision</u>** - Matthew 18:21-22 - *Then Peter came to Him and said, "Lord, how often shall my brother sin against me, and I forgive him? Up to seven times?" Jesus said to him, "I do not say to you, up to seven times, but up to seventy times seven.*

There are Two Components of Forgiveness

6. **First - there is a <u>Heart</u> Component** or Vertical Component. (Romans 12:18)

7. **The Second Component of Forgiveness** is the <u>Transactional</u> or <u>Relational</u> component. (Matthew 18:15)

4 Promises of Forgiveness

1. I will not <u>dwell</u> on this incident

2. I will not <u>bring</u> this incident up and <u>use</u> it <u>against</u> you

3. I will not <u>talk</u> to <u>others</u> about this incident

4. I will not allow this incident to <u>stand between</u> us or <u>hinder</u> our personal relationship

SEXUAL INTEGRITY

Lesson #8 – Classroom Discussion Answers

Sexual Integrity and Sexual Impurity

Sexual Addictions

1. <u>God</u> does not tempt us to sin, we are tempted by <u>evil</u> when we are <u>drawn</u> away by our own <u>desires</u> and enticed. (James 1:13-14)

2. <u>When</u>, not if we are <u>tempted</u> to sin, God will make a way of escape for us. (1 Corinthians 10:13)

3. We sin against God <u>sexually</u>, when we look <u>lustfully</u> with our eyes at another person. (Matthew 5:27-28)

The Bible tells us to flee sexual immorality because:

4. Every sin that a man does is outside the body, but he who commits <u>sexual immorality</u> sins against his own <u>body</u>. (1 Corinthians 6:18)

5. Whoever <u>commits</u> sin is a <u>slave</u> to sin. (John 8:34)

The Mind and the Heart

6. Cast down arguments and every <u>high thing</u> that exalts itself against the knowledge of God, bringing every <u>thought</u> into <u>captivity</u> to the <u>obedience</u> of Christ. (2 Corinthians 10:5)

7. To be <u>carnally</u> minded is <u>death</u>, but to be <u>spiritually</u> minded is <u>life</u> and peace. (Romans 8:6)

8. We must set our minds on things <u>above</u> not on things on the <u>earth</u>. (Colossians 3:2)

9. Guard your <u>heart</u> by <u>meditating</u> on the <u>Word</u> to protect yourself from sexual immorality. (Proverbs 4:23, Matthew 15:19, Psalm 119:11)

10. If we <u>confess</u> our sins, His is faithful and just to <u>forgive</u> us our sins and to <u>cleanse</u> us from all unrighteousness. (1 John 1:9)

SPIRITUAL WARFARE

Lesson #9 – Classroom Discussion Answers

Primary weapons of the enemy – how he wages battle against us

1. **Deception** – the stronghold is an incorrect thinking pattern that stems from believing something that is not true

2. **Temptation** – when we are enticed to sin – devil makes it 'look good'

3. **Accusation** – devil then condemns you for what he enticed you to do

How are the weapons of the devil used to attack a person (particularly a Christian) in the area of habitual sin, and how do we fight back?

1. **Deception** – I have experienced negative things in my life and therefore I am not loved

    a. **Belt of Truth** - Truth of God's Word – Jeremiah 31:3 – *"...I have loved you with an everlasting love; Therefore with lovingkindness I have drawn you."*
    b. **Sword of Spirit** - God's Word
        i. John 3:16 – *"For God so loved the world that He gave His only begotten Son, that whoever believes in Him should not perish but have everlasting life."*
        ii. Isaiah 43:18-19 – ¹⁸*"Do not remember the former things, Nor consider the things of old.* ¹⁹*Behold, I will do a new thing, Now it shall spring forth; Shall you not know it? I will even make a road in the wilderness And rivers in the desert."*

2. **Temptation** – to believe that whatever the enemy is dangling before me as an unholy temptation is what I need and want.

    a. Satan makes this sin look good but we know that it is not God's will for our lives.
    b. James 4:7 says, *"Therefore submit to God. Resist the devil and he will flee from you."* Submit to the truth of God's word and resist the temptations of the enemy of your soul.

3. **Accusation** – if you submit to the temptation and go where you have no business going, the devil then accuses you and condemns you for your sin.

    a. **Shield of Faith** – use this weapon to extinguish the fiery darts of the enemy
    b. **Repent** and ask Jesus for forgiveness – 1 John 1:9 says, *"If we confess our sins, He is faithful and just to forgive us our sins and to cleanse us from all unrighteousness."*
    c. **Jesus does not condemn** - John 3:17 - *For God did not send His Son into the world to condemn the world, but that the world through Him might be saved.*

You have the <u>authority</u> to cast out demons. (Luke 10:19)

THE HEART

Lesson #10 – Classroom Discussion Answers

Idolatry

When we enter into an unhealthy emotional relationships with other people, we turn him/her and our relationship with him/her into an idol. This is sin in eyes of God. His Word gives us instruction about what we are to do in this instance; similar to other types of sin we have studied over the past couple of weeks.

1. We are <u>cursed</u> when we trust in <u>people</u> to give us strength and allow our <u>hearts</u> to <u>depart</u> from God. (Jeremiah 17:5)

2. We are to <u>flee</u> from <u>idolatry</u>. (1 Corinthians 10:14)

Hardening of the Heart

Some people, as a result of past hurts in their lives, have allowed their hearts to turn to stone as a defense mechanism to protect them from further hurt.

3. God will take the heart of <u>stone</u> out of your <u>flesh</u> and give you a new heart of flesh. (Ezekiel 36:26

OUR AUTHORITY IN CHRIST TO ROUT DEMONS

Lesson #11 – Classroom Discussion Answers

1. The <u>war</u> we fight and the <u>weapons</u> we use are not of this world, they are <u>spiritual</u>. (2 Corinthians 10:3-5)

2. To demolish the <u>strongholds</u> that keep us in bondage to sin, we have to <u>trust</u> God and change our <u>thinking</u>. (2 Corinthians 10:3-5)

3. We are to <u>endure hardship</u> as a good soldier, <u>pleasing</u> to Jesus Christ. (2 Timothy 2:3-4)

4. I am God's <u>child</u> and have already <u>overcome</u> the enemy because I have God in me and therefore I am <u>stronger</u> than the enemy who is in the world. (1 John 4:4)

FORGIVENESS - PART II

Lesson #12 – Classroom Discussion Answers

1. If Jesus makes you <u>free</u> from your sin, you are <u>free</u> indeed. (John 8:36)

2. We are <u>redeemed</u> by the blood of Jesus and are granted <u>forgiveness</u> of our sins according to the riches of His <u>grace</u>. (Ephesians 1:7)

3. While Jesus stands ready to forgive us of our sins, there are some prerequisites to receiving God's forgiveness. What do you suppose they are?

   - <u>Repent</u> – express sincere regret – true change of heart and turning away from sin (Matthew 9:13)
   - <u>Confess</u> – tell God what we are repenting for (1 John 1:9)
   - <u>Ask</u> – we must expressly ask God for forgiveness (1 John 5:14-15, Matthew 21:22)

4. When Jesus forgives our sins, He chooses <u>not</u> to <u>remember</u> our <u>sin</u>. (Hebrews 8:12)

5. God stands ready to <u>forgive</u> us, and He is <u>merciful</u> and <u>loving</u> towards us. (Psalm 86:4-5)

6. Nothing can <u>separate</u> us from the <u>love</u> of God. (Romans 8:38-39)

www.ingramcontent.com/pod-product-compliance
Lightning Source LLC
Chambersburg PA
CBHW080726230426
43665CB00020B/2627